Tradition
and Growth

TRADITION
AND
GROWTH

A Study of Four
Mexican Villages

MANUEL AVILA

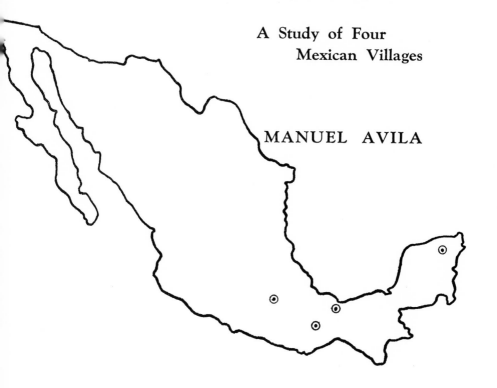

THE UNIVERSITY
OF CHICAGO PRESS

CHICAGO AND LONDON

Standard Book Number: 226-03245-0
Library of Congress Catalog Card Number: 73-86134

THE UNIVERSITY OF CHICAGO PRESS, CHICAGO 60637
THE UNIVERSITY OF CHICAGO PRESS, LTD., LONDON

To Kathy
Carol
Louise

The position of a nation,
in respect of its neighbours,
is analogous to the
relation of one of its provinces
to the others,
or of the country to the town;
it has an interest in their prosperity
being sure to profit
by their opulence

JEAN-BAPTISTE SAY
A Treatise on Political Economy

Contents

Tables

Preface

This is a story of four Mexican villages: Chan Kom, Soteapan, Mitla, and Tepoztlán. The first is a society of Maya Indians not far from the great city of their ancestors, Chichén Itzá. The second is another peasant society, nestled in the heart of the Sierra Madre Oriental. The third is a community of Indians with no less illustrious ancestors than the first; they are descendants of the Zapotecan architects who built the famous temples of Mitla. The last, and largest of the four, is a village that battled Cortés when he advanced against the ramparts of the Aztec Empire.

The history of these villages would make fascinating reading; the account of the whys and wherefores of vanished societies is always intriguing. This book is more prosaic. It is not concerned with their past but with their present. In a country modernizing at a rapid pace, these four villages belong to what may be called its traditional sector, and the question that I want to pose is whether they are going to be modern too—whether they are going to share in the wave of progress agitating Mexico or whether they are going to be left behind, undisturbed to reminisce about days gone by.

The realization that a reciprocity exists between village and village, or between village and metropolis, was clear to the wordly philosophers of old. They understood that a bond exists between country and town, between city and hinterland. To them prosperity in a country had no reality unless it was real in all provinces and regions of the country. These ideas, unfortunately, have been lost sight of. The proposition that the well-being of a nation cannot be separated from the well-being of all its parts seems to have been forgotten. Hence, national growth—to place the issue in more modern terms—is usually considered independently of the spatial dimension in which it should take place. Not much attention is drawn away from the foci where growth is most evident: the cities. Not much attention is given to the backwoods that support great numbers of people.

This is a myopic stance, for the country may be missing something important by not achieving a closer integration of these regions. This study explores such a possibility in the case of Mexico. It uses a small piece of recent village history to see whether traditional societies deserve to be forgotten. It is possible that instead of being pools of stagnation, as some allege, they are reservoirs of untapped wealth waiting to make their contribution.

The author acknowledges a special debt of gratitude to the investigators who preceded him in the study of the villages— a debt that must be acknowledged in memoriam in two cases: to Robert Redfield (dec.) and Alfonso Villa for their studies of Chan Kom, to Elsie Clews Parsons (dec.) for her study of Mitla, to Robert Redfield again and Oscar Lewis for their studies of Tepoztlán, and to George M. Foster for his study of Soteapan.

A debt is also acknowledged to Professor Wilfred Malenbaum, who first directed the work on which the study is based, and to Professors F. G. Adams, Dorothy S. Brady, and Sidney Weintraub, University of Pennsylvania, all of whom influenced in a special way the development of the author's ideas.

Mr. Angel Palerm, former director of the Department of Social Affairs, Pan American Union, was extremley helpful in making available case studies of Latin American villages and in providing the author with personal references that facilitated his fieldwork in Mexico. In Yucatán, Professor Alfredo Barrera, director of the Instituto Yucateco de Antropología e Historia, gave him the benefit of his vast knowledge of Maya culture and eased the physical hardships that residence in the hinterland of the Yucatecan peninsula imposes on a field researcher. To both of them the author is most grateful.

Tradition
and Growth

1
The Traditional-Modern Dichotomy

Travelers to developing countries are often struck by the sharp contrast that exists between the capital cities and the rural areas. The cities have most of the accoutrements of modern civilization: dazzling showpieces of modern architecture, fashionable stores, first-class hotels with well-known names; in sum, they very much resemble the cities of the most modern countries. By contrast, in the rural areas people live in a different world, one in which tradition and primitive patterns prevail and in which the level of living is much lower.

Thus between village and city there is a gap. The village represents the traditional past, the city represents the modern present, and between the two the separation is so marked that it can be thought of as a dichotomy—what in this study will be called the traditional-modern dichotomy.

It may be contended that between village and city there is a continuum rather than a dichotomy. In this there is truth; developing countries have not only a few big cities and many small villages but communities of other sizes in between. Yet, some cities so outdistance their rivals that to think of this disparity as a dichotomy seems justified. Geographers call these "primate" cities, that is, cities so important by virtue of their being the centers of government, education, industry, and finance that they far surpass other communities.[1]

1. See Mark Jefferson, "The Law of the Primate City," *Geographical Review*

This dichotomy has not failed to make its mark. Some economists take it to be one of the distinguishing characteristics of emerging countries.[2] Others have been led by it to the concept of dualism. Boeke, for example, grounds his theory of dualism precisely on the disparity between city and countryside.[3] Lewis cites India as an example of a dual society in which there is a widening gap between "an industrializing urban minority" and a "stagnating rural community."[4] Hirschman notes that one of the features of the industrialization process is "the prolonged coexistence and cohabitation of modern industry and of preindustrial, sometimes neolithic, techniques," and he adds that "this 'dualistic' character of developing countries is to be noted not only with respect to methods of production and distribution; it exists also in attitudes and in ways of living and doing business."[5]

From a geographical point of view, tradition and modernity need not be widely separated; traditional villages are frequently found in proximity to cities. The contrast between tradition and modernity, moreover, can be observed along

29, no. 2 (April 1939): 226. According to Jefferson, "seconds are not next to, but far, far less in size than their primates." B. J. L. Berry in "Some Relations of Urbanization and Basic Patterns of Economic Development," *Urban Systems and Economic Development* (Eugene: University of Oregon, School of Business Administration, 1962), pp. 1-15, goes further and states that there tends to be an inverse relationship between primacy on the one hand and development and size of country on the other; primacy diminishes as a country develops and as the size of the country gets larger. In the latter publication (pp. 17-20), C. E. Browning also discusses primacy ("Primate Cities and Related Concepts") and cites Mexico City as an example of a primate city whose dominance works to the disadvantage of the country.

2. P. T. Bauer and B. S. Yamey, *The Economics of Under-developed Countries* (Chicago: University of Chicago Press, 1957), p. 7; W. A. Lewis, "Economic Development with Unlimited Supplies of Labor," in *The Economics of Underdevelopment*, ed. A. N. Agarwala and S. P. Singh (London: Oxford University Press, 1958), p. 408; Gunnar Myrdal, *An International Economy* (New York: Harper and Brothers, 1956), pp. 3, 167.

3. J. H. Boeke, *Economics and Economic Policy of Dual Societies* (New York: Institute of Pacific Relations, 1953), pp. 3-11, 15-16.

4. J. P. Lewis, *Quiet Crisis in India* (Washington, D. C.: Brookings Institution, 1962), p. 4.

5. A. O. Hirschman, *The Strategy of Economic Development* (New Haven: Yale University Press, 1958), pp. 52, 125-26, 184.

different spatial dimensions. Within the borders of a country the contrast may exist between village and city, or betweeen an entire rural region (state, province, etc.) and an urban region. Similarly, a dichotomy can be said to exist on a world-wide basis between the advanced countries and the emerging countries.

Few would question that the latter countries are split along the lines suggested, but the interregional split can also be easily detected in the most advanced countries.[6] However, some distinctions need to be made; first, the interregional gap is much more pronounced in developing countries than in advanced countries. To illustrate, in the United States in 1965 the average per capita personal income[7] of the richest state was 2.1 times that of the poorest state,[8] but the corresponding ratio for Brazil in 1960 was 10.1,[9] and in this same year in Mexico the ratio of average per capita GNP between the richest and the poorest state was 11.6.[10] Ratios similar to

6. See Benjamin Higgins, *Economic Development* (New York: W. W. Norton & Company, 1968), p. 236; E. L. Ullman, "Regional Development and the Geography of Concentration," *Papers and Proceedings of the Regional Science Association* (1958), p. 179; and J. R. Hicks, *Essays in World Economics* (Oxford: Clarendon Press, 1959), p. 162. Williamson theorizes that interregional disparities rise during the early stages of development but that later on, when the more mature stages are reached, convergence takes place. See J. G. Williamson, "Regional Inequality and the Process of National Development: A Description of the Patterns," *Economic Development and Cultural Change* 13, no. 4, pt. 2 (July 1965).
7. In what follows, per capita income is used as a measure of interregional disparities. Henceforth the terms *traditional-modern dichotomy* and *interregional inequality* will be used interchangeably in order to avoid repetition.
8. U. S. Department of Commerce, *Survey of Current Business* 46, no. 8, (August 1966), table 2, p. 13. The ratio is based on Connecticut's per capita personal income of $3,401 and Mississippi's corresponding figure of $1,608. A second illustration of the gap in advanced countries is Japan where the ratio is reported to be 3.3. See Saburo Okita, "Regional Planning in Japan Today," in *The State and Economic Enterprise in Japan,* ed. W. W. Lockwood (Princeton: Princeton University Press, 1965), p. 626.
9. Instituto Brasileiro de Geografia e Estatística, Conselho Nacional de Estatística, *Anuário estatístico do Brazil, 1964,* p. 266, shows that the state of Guanabara—where Rio is located—had a per capita income of 77,963 cruzeiros, whereas the per capita income of the state of Piaui—found in the poor Northeast region—was only 7,710 cr.
10. P. L. Yates, *El desarrollo regional de Mexico* (Mexico: Banco de Mexico,

the latter can be found in European countries. For example, it is reported that in Yugoslavia in 1957 the per capita income of the advanced areas was 10 times that of the backward areas.[11] But even in Sweden, as Myrdal notes, great inter-regional disparities can still be found.[12]

A second distinction is that in the richer countries inter-regional inequalities seem to be diminishing, while in the poorer countries they have been increasing.[13] Furthermore, in developed countries the prosperous regions are more wide-spread. As a rule developed countries have a relatively large number of cities, or centers of growth, whereas underdeveloped countries often have only one primate city.

A fourth distinction may be suggested; in resource-rich countries, poor regions can be found which were once prosperous, whereas in poorer countries—especially in monoproductive ones—the poor regions are those that, more often than not, have never been developed. Many Latin American countries fit into the latter category; a country like Brazil, however, fits into the first category. Two sugar-producing states of Brazil, Bahia and Pernambuco, that belong to what is now the impoverished Northeast were in the late seventeenth century the most populous and wealthy regions of the country.[14]

It may be added that most cities of poor countries have been centers of modernity for a long time. The present capi-

---

1961), tables 14 and 15, pp. 62-63. Yates reports a per capita GNP of 11,900 pesos for the state of Baja California Norte, whereas the corresponding figure for the state of Oaxaca is only 1,022 pesos. The question of whether the per capita GNP for Oaxaca is as low as Yates indicates is explored in the last chapter of the present study.

11. S. H. Robock, "Regional and National Economic Development in India," *Papers and Proceedings of the Regional Science Association* (1960), p. 66.

12. G. Myrdal, *Economic Theory and Under-developed Regions* (London: Gerald Duckworth & Co., 1959), p. 32.

13. United Nations, Department of Economic and Social Affairs, *Economic Survey of Europe in 1954* (Geneva, 1955), pp. 138-42.

14. See Caio Prado, Jr., *The Colonial Background of Modern Brazil* (Berkeley: University of California Press, 1967), pp. 32-35. See also J. F. Normano, *Brazil, A Study of Economic Types* (Chapel Hill: University of North Carolina Press, 1935), p. 7.

tal cities of Latin America, for example, have been centers of this type since colonial times—again with the exception of Brazil. These cities, moreover, tend to introduce the latest manifestations of modernity shortly after they appear in the advanced countries. Electricity, motor vehicles, computers, and the stock ticker are examples that come readily to mind, but the list could be expanded. Today many such cities have television, and on their streets one occasionally sees rustically dressed peasants carrying transistor radios.[15]

What, it may now be asked, are the factors that account for the emergence of interregional inequalities? One factor is natural resources. When a resource or raw material is in demand its exploitation brings prosperity to some privileged regions; as it declines in importance the regions which were prosperous may also decline. Thus in the case of Brazil the centers of prosperity rose and declined following a north-to-south direction as sugar, gold, cotton, cacao, rubber, and coffee took turns as the leading products.[16]

Strategic locations can also give rise to interregional inequalities. Locations with easy access to sources of power, to rivers, or to other means of communication have frequently been the sites of communities that have flourished.[17] Facility of transport seems to play a particularly important role. Progressive regions benefit from good means of transportation; conversely, inadequate transportation tends to perpetuate the backwardness of the remote regions, even when they are known to be rich in natural resources.

Finally, mere historical accidents are also causal factors.

15. References to the early introduction of modernity in India can be found in Wilfred Malenbaum, "Dilemmas of Development," in *Capital* (Calcutta), 20 December 1962, p. 6; *Prospects for Indian Development* (New York: Free Press of Glencoe, 1962), pp. 31-32; J. P. Lewis, *Quiet Crisis in India*, p. 4. Floyd Dotson and Lillian O. Dotson in "Urban Centralization and Decentralization in Mexico" (*Rural Sociology* 21, [1956]: 49) mention the early introduction in Mexico of the electric streetcar, the automobile, the motor truck, and the telephone.
16. See Normano, *Brazil*, pp. 14, 18-22.
17. See Hicks, *World Economics*, pp. 162-63.

Myrdal thinks that the simple fact that something successful
was once started in one place and not in another is sufficient
to explain the origin of growth centers, and hence the origin
of interregional inequalities.[18]

Whatever the historical accident or the original locational
advantage, as a center begins to grow a new and powerful
element enters into the generation of interregional inequality. This is a self-reinforcing momentum, engendered within
the center itself and powered by the work of both internal
and external economies[19]—a momentum which enhances the
original advantage thus allowing a process of cumulative
growth to take place, in some cases even after the disappearance of the condition that brought the center into being.[20]
As a center grows, it attracts new enterprises, which exert in
turn new powers of attraction: in a growing center industry
and trade find skilled labor, auxiliary services, sources of supply, a market, etc., and consequently both gravitate toward it.
Once the new centers are established they also become
sources of services and attract more industry and trade. It is
not long before this process also engenders the gap that will
be widened as the center continues to grow.

Government policy is a contributing factor. Repeatedly,
in one country after another, instances are found of taxes
and tariffs that favor the growth centers to the disadvantage
of the poor regions. The same is true of policies regarding
transportation and public utilities. Not uncommonly, prevailing rates are found which discriminate against the lagging
regions.

When brought together, resources, geography, cumulative

18. Myrdal, *Economic Theory*, pp. 26-27. See also United Nations, Department
of Economic and Social Affairs, *Economic Survey of Europe in 1953* (Geneva,
1954), p. 184.
19. Myrdal maintains that these economies and the free play of market forces
reinforce the continuous growth of a center "at the expense of other localities
and regions where instead relative stagnation or regression become the pattern." See Myrdal, *Economic Theory*, pp. 26-27 and passim. For the role of
external economies see also K. Mandelbaum, *The Industrialization of Backward Areas* (Oxford: Basil Blackwell, 1961), p. 4.
20. Hicks, *World Economics*, p. 163.

causation, and government are powerful forces that work toward inequality, but they do not go unchecked. Three "channels of equalization" work as countervailing forces: the movement of capital, the movement of goods and services, and the movement of labor. Capital movements, according to the explanation expounded by Hicks, operate as follows: a growing center, in search of the highest rate of profit, invests part of its savings outside itself, either in areas which can provide it with special materials, in areas having a latent geographical advantage, or in areas with lower costs. As these new areas attract capital from the growth center they are themselves able to prosper and become markets which draw industry and labor. In time they, too, become centers of wealth inducing corresponding advances in other regions. This according to Hicks is the "natural" way in which new centers develop and how, through the movement of capital, inequality is reduced.[21]

The equalizing role of the movement of goods and services is much more controversial. For decades it has been a subject on which the views of economists have clashed. A detailed investigation of the controversy is unnecessary for the aims of the study; however, a brief review of what can be considered its modern phase seems warranted. This dates from 1919 when, under a specific set of assumptions, Heckscher established that foreign trade leads to a maximization of national income.[22] He wondered at the fact that Ricardo's postulate of full factor immobility between countries had received little attention and thought that if, contrary to Ricardo's postulate, the factors of production were fully mobile, their prices would tend to be equalized throughout the world.

Heckscher's article had an impact on economists who were

21. Ibid., pp. 163-66.
22. E. F. Heckscher, "The Effect of Foreign Trade on the Distribution of Income," in *Readings in the Theory of International Trade* (Philadelphia: Blackiston Co., 1950), p. 272. For a historical account of this and related subjects see Jagdish Bhagwati, "The Pure Theory of International Trade: A Survey," *Economic Journal* 74, no. 293 (March 1964): 1-84.

interested not in international but in domestic trade. Williams was led to believe that it was Ricardo's other postulate —about the free mobility of factors within countries—that was less tenable and therefore in greater need of defense.[23] To Williams the evidence showed that until the middle of the eighteenth century large commerce had been international; some countries had had so little internal trade that he thought the productive factors had moved more freely between countries than within them. He also observed that interregional differences did not seem to disappear.[24]

In the thirties, Ohlin introduced the proposition that international trade serves as partial substitute for factor movements and concluded that it leads to partial equalization of factor prices.[25] Samuelson pursued this further and proved that not only partial but full equalization occurs, both relatively and absolutely.[26] The assumptions supporting Samuelson's conclusion are not ground on observation, and therefore his proof has met with skepticism regarding its applicability to the real world.[27] Some writers have recognized its merit

23. For a criticism of Ricardo's postulates see J. E. Cairnes, *Some Leading Principles of Political Economy* (reprint ed., New York: Augustus M. Kelley, 1967), pp. 302-5.
24. J. H. Williams, "The Role of International Trade Reconsidered," in *Readings in the Theory of International Trade,* pp. 256-57. Williams mentions that Cliffe Leslie "found within England, France, Belgium, and Germany, local diversities of all sorts; some which had persisted for centuries and some which were the product of the new nineteenth-century economic activity, in which foreign trade played a major part."
25. Bertil Ohlin, *Interregional and International Trade* (Cambridge: Harvard University Press, 1933), chaps. 1, 2, and app. 1. The proof has come to be known as the Heckscher-Ohlin factor price equalization theorem.
26. P. A. Samuelson, "International Trade and the Equalization of Factor Prices," *Economic Journal* 58, no. 230 (June 1948): 163; and "International Factor Price Equalization Once Again," *Economic Journal* 59, no. 234 (June 1949): 181.
27. See Hicks, *World Economics,* pp. 260-69; Svend Laursen, "Production Functions and the Theory of International Trade," *American Economic Review* 42, no. 4 (September 1952): 540; Fritz Machlup, "Professor Samuelson on Theory and Realism," *American Economic Review* 54, no. 5 (September 1964): 733, and reply; Folke Hildgerdt, "Uses and Limitations of International Trade in Overcoming Inequalities in World Distribution of Population and Resources," *Proceedings of the World Population Conference, 1954* (New York: United Nations) p. 52. It should be noted that the assumptions did not originate with Samuelson but can be traced to Ohlin.

as a normative or hypothetical construct, but others have even questioned its logical validity.[28]

While the equalization theorem has dealt mainly with whether international trade brings about convergence of factor prices, the operation of trade at the national level has also been analyzed; and lately the question posed is not whether trade results in convergence of factor prices but whether it results in equalization of per capita income.[29] Myrdal, among others, takes a pessimistic view and comes to the conclusion that trade, far from being a channel of equalization, is a medium through which the rich regions become richer while the poor regions become poorer. Myrdal's thesis at the national level is paralleled by Prebisch's thesis at the international level, the main contention of which is that the fruits of trade are transferred from the peripheral, or poor, countries to the industrial, or rich, countries.[30] In somewhat less depressing terms, Hicks concedes that trade is a force working toward interregional equality, but nevertheless he expresses doubt as to whether trade can operate effectively by itself.[31]

The third channel of equalization, the movement of labor, seems to be the most effective; however, a general proposition concerning its effects cannot be formulated without considering the direction followed by the movement, the economic condition of the labor and regions involved, and the time span in which the effects of the movement are allowed to

28. S. F. James and I. F. Pearce, "The Factor Price Equalization Myth," *Review of Economic Studies* 19, pt. 2, no. 49 (1951-52): 111-20. These authors point out that in effect Samuelson's exercise amounts to an assertion of what it tries to prove and that, except under unlikely assumptions, it is neither more difficult nor less plausible to set up conditions under which trade leads to divergence of factor prices.
29. Bernard Okun and Richard W. Richardson, "Regional Income Inequality," *Economic Development and Cultural Change* 9, no. 2 (January 1961): 130, point out that a tendency toward equalization of factor prices need not mean a tendency toward equalization of per capita income.
30. Myrdal, *Economic Theory*, pp. 27-28; Raul Prebisch, "Commercial Policy in the Underdeveloped Countries," *Papers and Proceedings of the American Economic Association* 49, no. 2 (May 1959): 251-73.
31. Hicks, *World Economics*, p. 170.

work themselves out.[32] For a given labor movement the productivity changes that result are the critical issue. To illustrate, under the conditions found in actual practice—labor moving from the poor to the rich regions—equalization will come about if the movement makes possible productivity increases in the poor region large enough to more than offset whatever gains may accrue to the rich region. If the situation is the opposite, that is, if the labor that leaves the poor area is the most productive and so is able to make large contributions to output in the modern center, equalization will not occur—particularly if the movement seriously impairs the ability of the poor region to increase or even maintain its output. Of course labor is not homogeneous, and if the labor that moves to the rich center is the least productive such a movement may accomplish nothing more than to lower the per capita income of the rich region. In the latter case some equalization would undoubtedly take place, at the expense of the rich region.

Where the time element is concerned, it is necessary, as Okun and Richardson point out, to make a distinction between long-run and short-run effects. The immediate effect of a labor movement from a poor to a rich region is equalizing: the per capita income of the rich region goes down while that of the poor region goes up. In the long run, however, the per capita income of the poor region may go down while that of the rich region goes up. The reason is that the labor that moves to the rich region may eventually find employment and become productive, whereas the labor that remains in the poor region, either because it consists of the old or the less ambitious workers, may eventually produce a smaller output. Thus in the long run equalization would not occur.

The fact that interregional inequalities persist for long periods of time indicates that the channels of equalization either do not work or are not effective. Whichever the case,

32. See Okun and Richardson, "Regional Income Inequality," p. 143.

it seems that at best they can be only moderately successful. Functioning by themselves—for example, under free-market conditions—these channels, especially in poor countries, may lead to no equalization at all. In some instances they may even act in a perverse fashion, or the positive effect of one may be cancelled by the negative effect of the others.[33] Then, there is the matter of government policy. As previously indicated, taxes, tariffs, or policies in the fields of transportation and public utilities may discriminate against the poor regions thereby making the task of the channels of equalization even more burdensome. Of course government policy need not always work against the poor regions; in the last few years those countries that have tried to establish a measure of regional equality have buttressed the work of the channels of equalization with a variety of governmental measures intended to help the poor regions.

Having examined the problem of the traditional-modern dichotomy, its origin, and the possible means toward its amelioration, the discussion can now be shifted to the content and methodology of the study. This is set against the background of present day Mexico and consists of a survey of four communities. These communities are scattered throughout the countryside and can be said to belong to Mexico's traditional sector. Therefore, they provide an inside vantage point from which to explore the theme under study —at least in Mexico's case.

It is hoped that by reviewing the experiences of these communities it will be possible to arrive at some conclusions concerning (1) the traditional-modern gap, (2) the nature of traditional societies, and (3) the contribution which these might make to national growth. Given the limited geographical scope and the limited sample of communities, it is of course not claimed that the conditions to be described typify

33. In Myrdal's view the three movements are the very media through which inequality is increased.

the traditional sector, nor that they apply to traditional
societies in general. In statistical terms, the sample, needless
to say, is too small, and then—as will be explained in the following chapter—the selection of the communities, few as
they were, was not random.

With these reservations in mind, much of a positive nature
remains. For instance, it was intended that actual phenomena
should come under observation; and this was accomplished.
Secondly, the experiences of the four communities may not
be unique, and therefore some of the findings may find applicability beyond the geographical boundaries of the study.
Lastly, the historical case-method used may well be, in the
language of the past few years, a "first approximation" to a
more comprehensive approach.

In the following four chapters, three decades of the communities' history are placed under review. The purpose is to
document the social and economic changes that occurred and
to set an empirical basis for their analysis. The historical
account is carried at two levels: some events relate to the
communities as a whole, others relate to individuals and
households. It is hoped that by following this approach
enough data will be brought out to assess the prospects of the
communities, to assess their past economic performance, and
to analyze the implications which this performance yields in
light of the issues raised thus far. Throughout, an effort is
made to bring out facts that may aid to understand the nature
of the communities. Traditional societies have rarely been
studied by economists and probably for this reason have been
an object of stereotypes not in accord with reality. This is the
more deplorable not only because misconceptions are allowed
to prevail but because traditional societies may be untapped
reservoirs of economic progress. For these reasons, there is a
need to question the popular notions. A brief clarification of
these notions will round out the scope of the study and put
in perspective some of the material of the following chapters.

Three notions concerning traditional societies have found

easy acceptance: the first is that traditional societies are over-burdened with surplus labor of which the marginal productivity is zero. The picture usually painted is one of agrarian societies teeming with people with little or nothing to do.[34] The second notion is that traditional societies are unable to generate savings. The people, it is believed, live at a subsistence level, and therefore saving is deemed impossible. The third notion, a corollary of the first two, is that traditional societies are stagnant.

Recent studies of underdeveloped countries show that, in the main, these notions are not supported by facts. Although references to the first abound in the literature and frequently include size estimates of the surplus labor, the conditions which make said labor surplus are seldom specified. Usually the contention is simply that farm labor with zero marginal productivity is plentiful—particularly of course in the under-developed countries—because it would be possible to remove large numbers of workers from the land without causing a fall in output. That this is not the case has been documented in a number of studies.[35] When labor has been withdrawn

34. A factor that may have contributed to the popularity of this notion is its use as an analytical construct. In some models, labor with zero marginal productivity is introduced as an assumption, which then seems to be taken as a fact. See W. A. Lewis, "Economic Development," p. 400; Gustav Ranis and J. C. H. Fei, "A Theory of Economic Development," *American Economic Review* 51, no. 4 (September 1961): 533. See also P. N. Rosenstein-Rodan, "Problems of Industrialization of Eastern and South-Eastern Europe," in *Economics of Underdevelopment,* ed. Agarwala and Singh, pp. 245-47; Mandelbaum, *Industrialization of Backward Areas,* pp. 1-2; Ragnar Nurkse, *Problems of Capital Formation in Underdeveloped Countries* (Oxford: Basil Blackwell, 1962), chap. 2, p. 32; Harvey Leibenstein, *Economic Backwardness and Economic Growth* (New York: John Wiley & Sons, 1962), pp. 40, 59-60.
35. See T. W. Schultz, "Latin-American Economic Policy Lessons," *"Papers and Proceedings of the American Economic Association,* 46, no. 2 (May 1956): 426-27; and *The Economic Test in Latin America,* New York State School of Industrial and Labor Relations, Cornell University, Bulletin 35 (August 1956), pp. 13-15. In Schultz's view there is no poor country in which even a withdrawal of only five percent of the agricultural labor force could take place, *ceteris paribus,* without a fall in output. See also B. Higgins, "Prospects for an International Economy," *World Politics* 9, no. 3 (April 1957): 466; E. E. Hagen, *The Economics of Development* (Homewood, Ill.: Richard D. Irwin, 1968), pp. 296-302.

from the land, *ceteris paribus,* a fall in output *has* occurred, even in such a populous country as India.[36]

If the conditions that make labor surplus were always made clear, there would be little room for misunderstanding. For instance, if it is assumed that labor is removed from the land, but coupled to this removal certain conditions are specified— such as the introduction of more up-to-date methods, the enlargement of the plots, or more efficient management—it is quite possible that agricultural output not only would fail to decrease but would actually go up. Under these conditions the presence of latent surplus labor would certainly have been revealed.[37] In the absence of such conditions, however, the contention that surplus labor is present is questionable indeed.

Like the first notion, the second is as popular as it is misleading. The contention is that traditional societies cannot accumulate the savings needed for capital investments, the

36. Morton Paglin in "Surplus Agricultural Labor and Development: Facts and Theories," *(American Economic Review* 55, no. 4 [September 1965]: 815) concludes that in India the existence of a redundant agricultural labor force with zero marginal productivity is more a myth than a fact. T. W. Schultz, *Transforming Traditional Agriculture* (New Haven: Yale University Press, 1964), chap. 4, arrives at the same conclusion after a study of India's epidemic of 1918-19. A similar situation seems to prevail in Korea; see B. Higgins's statement in *Economic Development and Cultural Change* 14, no. 2 (January 1966): 237. For estimates of the size of the surplus labor in India see W. A. Lewis, "Reflections on South-East Asia," *District Bank Review,* December 1952, p. 11; and *The Theory of Economic Growth* (London: George Allen and Unwin, 1961), pp. 326-27; A. J. Coale and E. M. Hoover, *Population Growth and Economic Development in Low-Income Countries* (Princeton: Princeton University Press, 1958), p. 116.

37. Thus in the case of Egypt, assuming the use of larger plots and some mechanization, estimates have been made which set the pre-World War II surplus farm population as high as 90 percent of the total. See Wendell Cleland, *The Population Problem in Egypt* (Lancaster, Pa.: Science Press Printing Company, 1936), p. 106; C. Issawi, *Egypt: An Economic and Social Analysis* (London: Oxford University Press, 1947), pp. 195-96; and D. Warriner, *Land and Poverty in the Middle East* (London: Royal Institute of International Affairs, 1948), pp. 3, 32-33. Estimates of the pre-World War II surplus agricultural populations of the countries of eastern and southern Europe can be found in W. E. Moore, *Economic Demography of Eastern and Southern Europe* (Geneva: League of Nations, 1945), pp. 61-69.

main obstacle being their low income level.[38] Here again, studies of traditional societies cast serious doubt on the validity of this contention. In India Lewis finds increasing evidence that "even average Indian villagers do a good deal of saving—in defiance, as it were, of a 'subsistence' level of income."[39] Similarly, Hagen notes that those who have grown up in western high-income societies probably feel that they could not live, let alone save, at the income level which they visualize in traditional societies; "but to assume" he adds, "that this is true of the people of those societies is gratuitous."[40] He points out that even in peasant societies the level of income is not so low that all of it is used for basic necessities.[41] The problem then is not whether saving takes place but the manner in which savings are used, for it is being realized that a large part of the savings of traditional societies go into such things as jewelry, gold, festivals, and idle cash balances. Moreover, it appears that even larger savings could be generated if the people were motivated to do so.

If one believes that the traditional sector has surplus labor and that it does not generate savings, it is easy to make the transition to the notion that it is stagnant. The stereotype in this case is indolent peasants, irresponsive to economic incentives. They are pictured as being uncalculating, uninterested, and unwilling or unable to produce larger outputs. As in the two previous cases, there are grounds to question this notion, for the fact is that far from being indolent, peasants have been found to be industrious and entrepreneurially minded, always looking for new ways of "turning

38. See, for instance, Nurkse, *Problems of Capital Formation,* p. 5.
39. J. P. Lewis, *Quiet Crisis in India,* pp. 34-35.
40. Hagen, *On the Theory of Social Change* (Homewood, Ill.: Dorsey Press, 1962), pp. 18, 38; and *The Economics of Development,* pp. 129-34.
41. Hagen, *Theory of Social Change,* p. 18. See also Schultz, "Latin American Economic Policy Lessons," p. 430; and N. S. Buchanan and H. S. Ellis, *Approaches to Economic Development* (New York: Twentieth Century Fund, 1955), p. 57.

a penny."[42] This does not mean that traditional societies are well-off or that their output could not be increased. One of the interesting characteristics of these societies, as will be made clear in chapter 6, is their remarkable potential for output expansion. Village farmers, however, may be kept from producing greater outputs by institutional factors— such as land tenure systems that prevent them from reaping the full benefit of their efforts—by climatic factors, including irregularity of rainfall, or by lack of technological know-how, to name a few.

So much for the background of the present study. Returning to the Mexican villages that provide its empirical backbone, one may ask: What does their historical analysis reveal concerning the traditional-modern dichotomy and the misconceptions just discussed? A preview of the most important findings can be anticipated at this point:

The four communities may be poor, but their relative rate of economic growth is higher than that of their more modern counterparts.

The communities offer good prospects for further growth even though various growth-retarding factors are at work.

Nonmaterial inputs have been largely responsible for the past progress of the communities and can still be largely responsible for their future progress.

The peasantry studied may exhibit nonpecuniary traits, but they are neither irresponsive to market phenomena nor uninterested in improving their condition.

42. See Sol Tax, *Penny Capitalism: A Guatemalan Indian Economy* (New York: Smithsonian Institute of Social Anthropology, 1953); Raymond Firth, "Capital, Saving, and Credit in Peasant Societies: A Viewpoint from Economic Anthropology," in *Capital, Saving, and Credit in Peasant Societies*, ed. R. Firth and B. S. Yamey, (Chicago: Aldine Publishing Company, 1956), pp. 21-24; Schultz, *Transforming Traditional Agriculture*, pp. 49, 128, 162; W. P. Falcon, "Farmer Response to Price Subsistence Economy: The Case of West Pakistan," *Papers and Proceedings of the American Economic Association* 54, no. 3 (May 1964): 580; and Raj Krishna, "Farm Supply Response in India-Pakistan: A Case of the Punjab Region," *Economic Journal* 73, no. 291 (September 1963): 477.

Both publicly and privately, the communities do save and use a large part of their savings for material improvements.

No evidence of labor with zero marginal productivity was found; signs may be detected of plain, not of disguised unemployment.

At low developmental levels the traditional sector may be able to bear most of the burden for its development, but at higher levels some outside capital is required.

The channels of equalization may help to close the traditional-modern gap, but the task cannot be left solely to their operation.

A substantial closing of Mexico's traditional-modern gap seems feasible, but the superior relative growth of the traditional sector must be of long duration.

Mexico's traditional-modern gap cannot be closed by transferring rural labor to industry or to the modern agricultural sector.

Growth at the national level will be more apparent than real unless it encompases growth in the traditional sector.

The full discussion of these findings is presented in chapter 6; the next four chapters throw the spotlight on the villages.

2
Aspects of
Mexican Rural Life
in the Thirties

As mentioned in the preceding chapter, the empirical basis of the study rests on the case histories of four Mexican villages. These villages are located in different regions of the country, they vary in size, and they have different natural resources. But they have one feature in common; they are traditional societies and therefore their experiences are of the essence to this study.

The investigative method followed consists of surveying the villages at two points in time, noting the changes that occurred in the interim. Thus, it basically requires two sets of observations, one for what might be called the base period, the other for what might be called the terminal period. In the present case the early thirties constitute the base period, the early sixties the terminal period. In the selection of communities the possible choices were limited because so few have been the subject of economic investigations. Then, communities that had been studied at two different points in time were needed, which introduced a further restriction. In the end, availability of data became the critical issue and dictated the actual selection.

The four villages chosen were first studied by ethnologists and sociologists. From their surveys, and from auxiliary sources, enough information has been assembled to determine the economic condition of the villages in the base period. The investigation of the terminal period was the author's responsibility. It consisted of a field survey of the villages in the spring of 1964 and included a limited number of household interviews to determine income, expenditures, savings, investment, and other data related to the objectives of the study.

The results of these interviews are presented in chapter 5. Added to the material of chapters 3 and 4, they provide a historical record of the most important changes that took place during the thirty years under review. The analysis of these changes is the task of chapter 6. There the main threads of the study are brought together to determine the relative economic position of the villages with respect to the country as a whole and to the country's modern sector, and also to allow an appraisal of the progress achieved by the villages between the base and terminal periods. The study concludes by focusing again on the traditional-modern gap, taking into account the development potential of the villages and the role which they might play in the growth of the nation as a whole. It is hoped that throughout the study enough facts are brought to light to aid in the understanding of traditional societies.

Information about the base-period surveys is given in table 1: the names of the four villages, the original researchers,[1] and the years during which field research was conducted.

As table 1 indicates, the original village studies were done, for the most part, around 1930. A rapid survey of the country reveals that at that time Mexico had a total population of some 16.5 million people, 66.6 percent of whom lived in rural areas.[2] The number of those gainfully employed amounted to some 5.1 million persons, 70.2 percent of whom

---

1. The titles of their works are the following: Robert Redfield, *Tepoztlán: A Mexican Village* (Chicago: University of Chicago Press, 1930); E. C. Parsons, *Mitla: Town of the Souls* (Chicago: University of Chicago Press, 1936); Robert Redfield and Alfonso Villa, *Chan Kom: A Maya Village* (Chicago: University of Chicago Press, 1934); and G. M. Foster, *A Primitive Mexican Economy*, Monographs of the American Ethnological Society (Locust Valley, N. Y.: J. J. Augustin, 1942). The additional sources of information used for the survey of the base period are indicated at appropriate places in the text.
2. These and some of the following data are found in *Quinto censo de población, 1930* (Mexico: Dirección General de Estadística). The rural population is defined as that living in communities of 2,500 inhabitants or less.

were engaged in agriculture.[3] So large an agricultural sector
posed a serious problem because good agricultural land was
—and still is—scarce. Large areas are mountainous, others
are completely arid, and others lack adequate rainfall.[4] Only
about one-third of the country can be considered level.[5]
There are flat lands at high altitudes, but they are difficult
to irrigate because they lack streams. In lands where streams
are found "the drop in altitude is so sudden that the streams
tend to become veritable torrents during the rainy season

TABLE 1

The Base-Period Surveys

VILLAGE	RESEARCHER(S)	YEAR(S) OF FIELD RESEARCH
Tepoztlán	Robert Redfield	1926-27
Mitla	Elsie C. Parsons	1929-33
Chan Kom	Robert Redfield and Alfonso Villa	1931
Soteapan	George M. Foster	1941

and to revert to dry gullies in the wintertime."[6] Steep
gradients are characteristics of one-fourth of the land, but
only some of them are productive, supporting at best forests
or pastures.[7] Furthermore, since more than one-half of
Mexico lies at altitudes exceeding 3,000 feet, crop damage

3. Agricultural occupations included crop production, stock raising, forestry,
fishing, and hunting. The rest of the labor force was employed as follows:
14.4 percent in industry (mining, petroleum, and manufacturing); 2.1 percent in transportation and communications; 5.3 percent in commerce; and
8.0 percent in all other occupations.
4. P. E. James in *Latin America* (New York: Odyssey Press, 1959), p. 602, reports that C. W. Thornthwaite devised a formula which showed the following
types of land: with adequate moisture in all seasons, 12.8 percent; deficient
in moisture throughout the year, 49.9 percent; deficient in moisture in the
summer, 1.4 percent; and deficient in moisture in the winter, 35.9 percent.
5. Ibid., p. 595.
6. N. L. Whetten, *Rural Mexico* (Chicago: University of Chicago Press, 1948),
p. 6.
7. Rene Dumont, "Mexico: The Sabotage of the Agrarian Reform," *New
Left Review,* no. 17 (Winter 1962), p. 46. Dumont quotes A. G. Gallardo as
the source of this information.

due to frost or hail is not uncommon. There are coastal areas in the southeastern part of the country that either have rivers or receive adequate rainfall; however, in the thirties they were ridden by malaria and lacked communications.

According to Simpson, in 1930 Mexico's cropland amounted to 7.4 percent of the total (3.6 percent under cultivation and 3.8 percent fallow), pasture lands accounted for 33.8 percent, forests accounted for 13.2 percent, and the remaining 45.6 percent represented all other lands.[8] He indicates that whereas the cropland in Mexico came to only 7.4 percent, in European countries the corresponding figure ranged between 20 and 40 percent. He also reports that 79.2 percent of the land was semiarid (i.e., it depended on seasonal rain), 11.6 percent was irrigated, and 8.9 percent was humid.[9] In short, these figures reveal that cropland with adequate irrigation was scarce indeed.

The most important crop since pre-Columbian times has been corn. In the agricultural year 1929–30, more land was given to corn cultivation than to all the other crops combined —"corn represented well over a third of the annual value of all crops produced."[10] Yet, in spite of this dependence on corn, Mexico's corn productivity was among the lowest in the world.[11] Beans too have always been very important in

8. The total land area reported by Simpson is 196.5 million hectares. See E. N. Simpson, *The Ejido, Mexico's Way Out* (Chapel Hill: University of North Carolina Press, 1937), p. 152. Since in what follows some of the data are reported in metric units, the following equivalences can be used to convert to the English system: 1 hectare = 2.47 acres; 1 sq. kilometer = 0.386 sq. miles; 1 kilometer = 0.62 miles; 1 meter = 3.28 feet; 1 kilogram = 2.2 pounds.

9. Ibid., p. 155. If the irrigated land and the humid land are combined into one class (which can be thought of as having adequate irrigation), they represent 3 million ha., i.e., only 1.5 percent of the total.

10. Ibid., p. 225.

11. Ibid., p. 160. Simpson notes that of forty-five countries for which average corn yields per hectare were reported in the *International Yearbook of Agricultural Statistics,* in the period 1923-27 Mexico ranked thirty-ninth. He adds that "on the average the yield per hectare of corn in Mexico is 6.1 metric quintals—1 quintal equals 100 kilograms, i.e., 220 lb.—compared, for example, with 22.0 quintals for Canada; 19.0 for Argentina; 16.2 for the United States; 15.5 for Italy; and 15.0 for Spain."

the Mexican diet, but like corn, this crop was also characterized by low productivity in the thirties.

Also important for consideration are some rural-urban
contrasts, that existed at the time of the early surveys. The
census of 1930 shows that Mexico City was the only city with
a population of more than one million. At the other extreme
there were 71,869 communities of 2,500 inhabitants or less.[12]
They represented 85 percent of all the communities and constituted the Mexican rural sector, which in the early thirties
was geographically and culturally isolated from the modern
sector, that is, from the capital of the country. Lack of roads
—the construction of which has always been difficult and
costly due to the mountainous nature of the country—and
other means of communication meant that in the rural areas
the peasants depended on the burro and on themselves for
the transport of wares to local markets. Access to national
markets was practically nonexistent.

Frank Tannenbaum noted that the Mexican village lacked
communication. It had neither train nor automobile. It had
neither telegraph nor telephone, and it had no post office.
In a study of 3,611 rural communities in the early thirties,
he found that although railway construction in Mexico dates
from the nineteenth century, 93.1 percent of these communities had no train communication.[13] According to him, over
86 percent of these communities had neither bus nor automobile transportation, and 72 percent of them obtained it
only by mule or horse. Moreover, in 45.8 percent of them it
was still common practice for people to carry their wares to
market on their backs.[14]

Tannenbaum also found that most crops were grown with
the aid of primitive tools. In many places not even the
wooden plow drawn by oxen was used, and in many others

12. *Anuario estadístico de los Estados Unidos Mexicanos, 1942* (Mexico:
Dirección General de Estadística), table 18, p. 38.
13. Frank Tannenbaum, "Technology and Race in Mexico," *Political Science
Quarterly* 61, no. 3, (September 1946), p. 375.
14. Ibid., p. 376.

slash-and-burn agriculture was still prevalent.[15] In 96.5 percent of the villages there were no tractors; in 54.3 percent of them, no steel plows; and in 29.6 percent, not even wooden plows—although draft animals were found in most villages.

The cultivated plots were rather small in size. For instance, the average plot in 76.3 percent of the villages was five hectares or less, and in only 16.2 percent was the average plot six hectares.[16] Of all the villages, only 7.2 percent had a local market, 54.4 percent of them had no stores, and 21.2 percent were reported as still using barter. Tannenbaum's survey also showed that there was a doctor in 2.2 percent of the villages and that 3 percent had a druggist.

For his survey Tannenbaum used questionnaires which were sent to the village teachers who acted as respondents. Thus each of the 3,611 villages had a teacher, but in this respect they were unusual because most villages in the country had neither a teacher nor a school. The villages surveyed had an average population of 520 persons while for the country as a whole the average village population was 300. Considering their size and the fact that they had a school, Tannenbaum wrote: "These communities are, therefore, closer to the larger world, and more in contact with it, are nearer to the urban centers, and have a greater measure of identity with modern Mexico. They are the richer and more 'modern' rural towns in the country."[17]

Set within the context of the national and rural conditions described in the preceding paragraphs, what was the situation of the four communities selected for study? Table 2 provides some information concerning their geographical locations.

15. Ibid., pp. 372-73. Tannenbaum notes that the use of primitive tools does not necessarily mean lack of knowledge of better ones; to some extent the tools or methods are determined by the nature (and the amount) of land.
16. Ibid., p. 372. The breakdown of the average plots by size was the following: in 20.6 percent of the villages, 1 ha.; in 20.4 percent, 2 ha.; in 14.6 percent, 3 ha.; in 11.2 percent, 4 ha.; in 9.5 percent, 5 ha.; and in 16.2 percent, 6 ha. No data were obtained for 7.5 percent of the villages.
17. Ibid., p. 366.

The four villages belong to states found in the central and southeastern part of Mexico. As the table indicates, these states, like the country at large, were predominantly rural. All the villages trace their origins to pre-Columbian times with the exception Chan Kom, which was founded in the 1880s by a small band of social discontents.[18]

TABLE 2

Geographical Characteristics of the Villages, 1930

VILLAGE	STATE WHERE LOCATED	DISTANCE TO STATE CAPITAL[a] (km.)	DISTANCE TO MEXICO CITY[a] (km.)	DISTANCE TO NEAREST RR STATION (km.)	STATE'S RURAL POPULATION[b] (%)
Tepoztlán	Morelos	20	90	5	74.8
Mitla	Oaxaca	40	380	12	81.9
Chan Kom	Yucatán	136	1,700	50	51.8
Soteapan	Veracruz	282	408	20	71.4
Mexico					66.6

NOTE: The conditions depicted by the data are those that prevailed in the villages in 1930, with the exception of Soteapan. For this village the table, and those that follow, show the conditions that prevailed in 1941.
[a] The distances to the state capitals and to Mexico City are those of currently existing roads.
[b] Population data from the census of 1930.

In the thirties, as mentioned previously, the great majority of the rural communities were poorly linked to the outside world. The four villages each had a railroad station more or less nearby. Table 2 shows that some of the distances to

18. Redfield and Villa report that the men who founded Chan Kom came there in search of land when the site was virgin territory. Gradually, other people arrived and Chan Kom became a small settlement in the bush. Disputes over the performance of various duties which the men of Chan Kom owed to another village—whence most settlers had come—and the desire to get aid from the state government to furnish an already built school—aid which was granted to *pueblos* ("towns") only—led to a decision to convert the settlement into a *pueblo*. The state government agreed and made an official grand of *ejidos* ("land") which Chan Kom took possession of in 1926. (See Redfield and Villa, *Chan Kom,* chap. 2.) It should be added that the ejido is land granted to an individual for his own use. It remains in his possession, or that of his heirs, as long as it is cultivated; the title, however, is kept by the ejido authorities, and hence an ejido cannot be sold by its holder.

the stations were rather short, but this does not mean that the communities were easily accessible. For instance, to go from Tepoztlán to the railroad station, a person had to cover a distance of only five kilometers, but these five kilometers meant an arduous climb on mountain trails requiring between one and two hours. Tepoztlán also had communication with its state capital, but again it was by difficult trails that could be traveled only on foot or on beasts of burden. Chan Kom was about fifty kilometers from the railroad terminal at Valladolid; however, in the thirties there was no direct communication between the two places. In fact, the only outlet that Chan Kom had was a twenty-kilometer bush trail that terminated at the archeological ruins of Chichén Itzá. Soteapan, situated on a mountainous region, had problems similar to those of Tepoztlán: it had communication with nearby railroad towns but these could be reached only by rough mountain trails. Of the four villages, Mitla was the one best located for communications. Advantageously situated at the end of a valley, it had a railroad station twelve kilometers away on the valley floor, and in addition it was joined to the state capital by an unpaved road.

It seems that all the villages, with the exception of Chan Kom, had mail delivery at the time of the original studies. Redfield reports that postal service by carrier to Tepoztlán was inaugurated in September 1926, and that the following year about a dozen letters arrived, and as many left, half of them being business letters.[19] Regular delivery of magazines and newspapers did not exist at that time. Parsons states that in Mitla there was a telephone in the municipal office (chronically out of order) and that there were six subscribers to a newspaper. She also reports that there was mail delivery and that one day the incoming mail consisted of twenty letters, five of which were for her.[20]

The population of the villages and other demographic

19. Redfield, *Tepoztlán*, pp. 145, 172.
20. Parsons, *Mitla*, pp. 163, 171, 466.

characteristics are given in table 3. The birth and deathrates of the villages, and of the country as a whole, were high. Two villages, Mitla and Chan Kom, had rates of population increase in excess of the national rate, caused in both cases by high village birthrates, inasmuch as their deathrates were

TABLE 3

Demographic Characteristics of the Villages, 1930

VILLAGE	POPULATION	BIRTHRATE (per 1,000)	DEATHRATE (per 1,000)	NATURAL POPULATION INCREASE (%)
Tepoztlán	2,580	43.8	22.2	2.1
Mitla	2,307	56.0	26.4	2.9
Chan Kom	250	56.0	26.4	2.9
Soteapan	580	....	....	....
Mexico	16.553[a]	49.4	26.6	2.3

Sources: Population figures from the census of 1930. Village birth and deathrates from the following sources: O. Lewis, *Life in a Mexican Village: Tepoztlán Restudied* (Urbana: University of Illinois Press, 1951), pp. 28-32; Parsons, *Mitla*, p. 10 (the birth and deathrates are based on her estimate of a Mitla population of 2,500 inhabitants); Redfield and Villa, *Chan Kom*, p. 13.
[a] Millions.

practically the same as the national rate. Tepoztlán had lower deathrates, but it also had lower birthrates with the net result that its population was increasing at a slower pace than that of the nation as a whole.

Concerning the population figures, it may be pointed out that in 1917 Chan Kom had only about 100 persons. Therefore, having reached a population of 250 by 1930 meant that it had more than doubled in thirteen years, with most of the increase being due to immigration.

Before the thirties the population of the other three villages seems to have remained stable for long periods of time. Mitla, for instance, had a population of 2,007 inhabitants in 1921, almost exactly the same population that it had in 1881

(2,000) .[21] In the case of Tepoztlán there are old records that
show that from the time of the Conquest there have been
two long population cycles with periods during which the
population has been larger than in modern times. It is not
known how many people inhabited Tepoztlán when the
Spaniards arrived; however, in 1560 (thirty-nine years after
Cortés conquered the village) a marked decline got under
way. The population went down to 5,865 in 1579 and by
1807 it was down to 2,540.[22] Then during the nineteenth
century it rose, reaching 3,416 in 1889, 3,968 in 1900, and
4,753 in 1910. The revolution started in 1910 and marked
the beginning of a second decline which reduced the population to 2,156 by 1921.[23] Then the trend was reversed once
more and by 1963 the figure had climbed to 5,350.[24]

Foster thinks that since the sixteenth century, stability
also characterized the population of Soteapan and its neighboring villages, at least until the twentieth century. As in the
previous case, it seems that Soteapan had a larger population
in colonial times. A work dating from the eighteenth century

21. The 1921 population figure is reported in the census of 1921. The
Mexican Revolution lasted from 1910 to 1920. During this period many
rural communities, and the country as a whole, lost population. Therefore,
in many instances the population figures for 1910 are higher than those for
1921, the latter being a year in which population was abnormally low. The
1881 population is reported by A. F. Bandelier in "An Excursion to Mitla,"
Papers of the Archeological Institute of America, American Series 2 (Boston:
Cupples, Upham, and Co., 1884), p. 278. A. G. Cubas in his *Diccionario
geográfico histórico y biográfico,* vol. 4 (Mexico, 1890), p. 105, records a
Mitla population of 2,160 for 1889.
22. The sources of these and the following data are: Oscar Lewis, *Life in a
Mexican Village: Tepoztlán Restudied* (Urbana: University of Illinois Press,
1951), pp. 26-29; census of 1900; and census of 1910. The 1889 population is
from Cubas, *Diccionario,* p. 297.
23. O. Lewis cites the following reasons for the first population decline:
epidemics, deaths in the mines of Cuautla and Taxco, and the departure of
a number of persons to avoid high taxes. Of course the revolution accounts
for the second decline; some people were killed and others fled to the state
capital or to Mexico City. Of those who fled many never returned to their
village.
24. This figure comes from a census taken by the local authorities.

indicates that in 1746 Soteapan had 358 families.[25] Later sources reveal a sharp decline. The census of 1910 reports a population of only 162 persons and in 1925 Blom found that there were no more than 20 families residing in the village. The main reason for this was the revolution and the unstable conditions brought on in its aftermath, such as the presence of rebels and bandits in the area.

TABLE 4

Cultural and Educational Characteristics of the Municipalities, 1930

MUNICIPALITY	LANGUAGE SPOKEN	NUMBER OF SCHOOLS	NUMBER OF TEACHERS	ILLITERATE POPULATION[a] (%)
Tepoztlán	Nahuatl	2	2	50[b]
Mitla	Zopotec	1	1	79[b]
Chan Kom	Maya	1	1	61[c]
Soteapan	Popoluca	..	..	69[b]
Mexico				59.3[c]

SOURCES: Data from the census of 1940 and the original village studies.
[a] Illiteracy means inability to read or write Spanish.
[b] Percentage of the adult population, considering as adults persons six years of age and over.
[c] Percentage of the adult population, considering as adults persons ten years of age and over; thus for Mexico the percentage is based on a total "adult" population of 11.7 million.

Since the twenties the population of the four villages has steadily and rapidly moved upward. Although table 3 shows that in the thirties their deathrates were relatively high, they were accompanied by birthrates that were much higher, and consequently a decline in deathrates meant that no obstacle stood in the way of drastic population increases.[26]

25. J. A. Villa-Señor y Sánchez, *Teatro americano: Descripción general de los reynos y provincias de la Nueva España y sus jurisdicciones* (Mexico, 1746), p. 366. This source is reported by Frans Blom and Oliver La Farge in *Tribes and Temples*, 2 vols. (New Orleans: Tulane University of Louisiana, 1926), 1:49-50.
26. O. Lewis, *Life in a Mexican Village*, p. 32, indicates that the birthrates of Tepoztlán—and probably those of the other villages—contain some error because not all births are recorded in the year of occurrence. When this

Table 4 gives some information about a different aspect of village life, the cultural level. Regarding the data of this table, it should be pointed out that the figures given under number of schools and number of teachers, as well as the illiterate population percentage shown for Chan Kom, pertain to the villages themselves, but the illiterate population percentages shown for Tepoztlán, Mitla, and Soteapan pertain to the three municipalities to which these villages belong. In each case the name of the municipality coincides with the name of the village, and all four villages are the seats of their municipalities. Frequently data can be found for municipalities but not for the separate communities that belong to them. As a rule the largest communities are chosen as municipal seats, and therefore, they contribute the largest weight to any municipal data. For this reason, the illiteracy rates of the villages themselves were probably quite close to the municipal rates shown by the table.

Since Spanish is the language used in Mexican schools, it can be inferred that the villages, having a school, must have had people who spoke Spanish. The illiteracy rates, however, show that those who could read or write Spanish were a minority. For the most part, Spanish was spoken only by the younger people; among adults there was a widespread use of the native languages. The national illiteracy rate was also high; but in contrast to the situation in the villages, for the Federal District (comprised mainly of Mexico City), the census of 1930 reported only twelve persons as speaking native languages exclusively. In Tepoztlán, Redfield observed that although about one-half of the adults could to some degree read and write Spanish, still "the Nahuatl language persists, and is spoken by nearly all the inhabitants. A number of young people speak it only as a second language of much

---

happens the delay is usually of only one year. Since this practice does not change from year to year, he thinks that the error is small. Deaths seem to be recorded in the year in which they occur.

less familiarity. On the other hand, nearly everyone speaks Spanish; there are a few old people who do not, and many to whom Spanish is the less familiar tongue."[27]

The two schools in Tepoztlán were government-supported, one by the state government, the other by the federal government. The Church operated a school at various times dating from the seventeenth century. The first secular school dates from the middle of the nineteenth century.[28] Redfield concluded that judged by the standards of the modern city, the people of Tepoztlán were illiterate. But he also pointed out that toward the end of the nineteenth century, coincident with the dictatorship of Porfirio Díaz, there was a period of brilliance during which a few Tepoztecans carried out various cultural activities, such as the publishing of local newspapers, the exploration of an archeological site, and the establishment of a museum.[29] All this, unfortunately, came to an end with the revolution of 1910.

Chan Kom, being a much younger village, had its first school in 1910. It was housed in a simple hut of wattle walls with a palm-leaf roof; however, it served not only Chan Kom but other neighboring settlements.[30] Redfield noticed that the language most widely spoken was Maya; Spanish was spoken by only 14 percent of the population, mainly in their dealings with outsiders or when they communicated with the teacher.[31]

Foster found two old references to the existence of a school in Soteapan; one goes as far back as 1831 and the other, the

27. Redfield, *Tepoztlán,* pp. 30, 170.
28. Ibid., pp. 170, 206.
29. Ibid., pp. 206-207.
30. Redfield and Villa, *Chan Kom,* pp. 25-26. Incidentally, the association between Redfield and Villa started in 1930 when Redfield, making an ethnological and sociological investigation in Yucatán, first visited Chan Kom; Villa was the school teacher at the time.
31. Ibid., pp. 15-17. Redfield and Villa caution against taking the percentage of illiterates shown by table 4 as accurate; they think that it understates the true number because in many cases literacy simply meant the ability to pronounce Spanish words without much understanding of their meaning.

census of 1869, reports that there was a school in the village and that only 17 persons, out of a population of 1,600, were able to read and write.[32] Foster does not make clear what the condition of the school was at the time of his visit. He states, however, that "a handful of men write a painful and stilted Spanish, but the culture remains essentially non-literate."[33] He also notes that contact with the outside during the twentieth century allowed most men to learn Spanish; the women, on the other hand, only knew a few words and could not converse in it. Hence, the Popoluca language was extensively used and the natives always spoke it among themselves.[34]

As table 4 shows, Mitla also had a school. Parsons recorded a number of observations about it, one being that it underwent various changes during her three visits to the village. At the time of her first visit in 1929 it had almost no equipment, attendance was low, and instruction was poor. At that time it was operated by the state government. From various references by Parsons to the schoolmaster, as well as from the number of children in attendance, it can be inferred that it had only one teacher.

In one of her later visits, Parsons noticed various improvements: it had been taken over by the federal government, it had acquired better equipment and better teachers—supplied from the state capital but paid by the village from a monthly tax on all males—and its attendance had doubled. In addition, there was a night school with an adult registration of 103 persons.[35] Except for a very few individuals, the inhabitants of Mitla considered themselves Indian and spoke the Zapotec language. Parsons observed an infiltration of Spanish words into the native language and this led her to conclude that "Obviously the Zapotecan language is pass-

32. Foster, *A Primitive Mexican Economy*, pp. 8, 14.
33. Ibid., p. 95, n. 4.
34. Ibid., p. 15. Blom and La Farge, *Tribes and Temples*, p. 53, note that there are many dialects known as Popoluca but that the variety spoken in Soteapan was Mixe-Zoque.
35. Parsons, *Mitla*, p. 91.

ing."[36] She gives no figures on literacy, but she relates that during an election, of 262 voters registered in one section of the village, less than 4 percent could write their names.[37]

Table 5 presents additional information about the four municipalities. The data show that the municipalities were big enough to accommodate their populations. The densities do not indicate pressure on the land at the municipal level,

TABLE 5

Demographic Characteristics of the Municipalities, 1930

MUNICIPALITY	SIZE (sq. km.)	NUMBER OF COMMUNITIES	POPULATION	DENSITY[a]
Tepoztlán	347	8	4,714	13.59
Mitla	280	4	4,109	14.46
Chan Kom[b]	24	. .	250	10.41
Soteapan	525	12	3,496	6.66
Mexico			16.553[c]	8.41

SOURCES: Data from the census of 1930, census of 1940, and from Redfield and Villa, *Chan Kom*, p. 29.
[a] Inhabitants per square kilometer.
[b] The data shown are for the village itself and not for the municipality.
[c] Millions.

nor at the national level. It seems that within the municipalities migration was quite limited; people tended to remain in their places of origin. Redfield believed that in Tepoztlán only about fifty men had been born outside the surrounding valley. On the other hand, Chan Kom, a much younger village, had few native adults. Most of them had come from settlements located within a radius of forty miles.

Land was easy to come by. With the exception of some plots privately held, the inhabitants of a municipality could legally use any piece of land located within the municipal boundaries. This right remains in force even today and in-

36. Ibid., pp. 15, 21.
37. Ibid., p. 156, n. 10.

cludes the use or appropriation of such land products as firewood, herbs, vines, and wild crops.

Next to be examined are various physical characteristics of the villages. The information is presented in table 6, which shows that in physical characteristics the villages are quite varied. On the one hand there is Chan Kom, found deep in the bush of the low and almost completely level Yucatán peninsula; and on the other there is Tepoztlán, located in a municipality where the terrain drops 6,800 feet

TABLE 6

Physical Characteristics of the Villages, 1930

VILLAGE	ALTITUDE[a]	NATURE OF SURROUNDING TERRAIN	CLIMATE	NON-RAIN WATER SOURCES
Tepoztlán	1,701	Mountainous	Temperate	Spring
Mitla	1,651	Valley	Temperate	Springs, wells
Chan Kom	20[b]	Rolling bush	Tropical	Well
Soteapan	499	Mountainous	Subtropical	Springs

[a] Meters above sea level.
[b] Approximate figure.

from the northern to southern boundary—a distance of seventeen miles. Mitla, as mentioned previously, lies at the end of a valley. It is surrounded on three sides by the sierra, and thus it serves as an outpost that links Oaxaca and the outside world to the west with mountain settlements to the north and the east.

The nature of the terrain and the availability of water from sources other than rain have been included in the table because of their importance in determining whether land could be cultivated. The table shows that the villages got their water from springs, wells, or both. Mitla had some springs of what the natives call "white water"—the color being produced by sediments that cause various stomach ailments. It also had three streamlets which, for the most part, were waterless during the dry season. On the banks of one of these streamlets there were several wells, and some houses also had wells. In addition there was a fountain near the church to which water was piped from a nearby spring of white water, "the only 'plumbing' in town."[38] Finally, there were two pumps, one at a corn-grinding mill and the other at the school.

Soteapan, situated on a mountain ridge, had springs on both sides. These formed small streams to which people came to bathe and get water. In Tepoztlán there was a spring from which water was piped to public fountains. There were also gullies that drained the water from the mountains during the rainy season, but at other times they were dry. Chan Kom had one of those natural wells that are found in Yucatán and which are formed by the collapse of the limestone shelf characteristic of the peninsula. In the thirties it supplied most of Chan Kom's water requirements.

While the villagers were able to obtain water for their households from the sources mentioned above, their agricultural lands depended on seasonal rain exclusively. In Mitla half a dozen men attempted to use primitive methods of irrigation, but the majority of the peasants in all four villages lacked irrigation facilities of any sort and so their most serious problem was scarcity of water. Adequate rainfall allowed crop estimates to be realized; drought, however, meant reduced harvests and in many cases no harvest at all. The problem was aggravated by the fact that practically every adult male was engaged in agriculture.

Table 7 gives an idea of the importance of agriculture by showing the limited scope of nonagricultural occupations. The original village studies do not provide data on the number of persons economically active. The small nonagricultural employment shown by the table, however, clearly indicates that agriculture was indeed the most important economic activity. Included in the number of nonagricultural occupa-

38. Ibid., p. 29.

tions are only those that resulted in income to the performer. Occupations such as marriage intermediary, musician, etc., which were performed occasionally and as a rule without pay, are not included. The number of those engaged in non-agricultural occupations was actually smaller than the num-

TABLE 7

Division of Labor in the Villages, 1926-33

VILLAGE	NUMBER OF NONAGRICULTURAL OCCUPATIONS	NUMBER ENGAGED IN NONAGRICULTURAL OCCUPATIONS	NUMBER OF COTTAGE INDUSTRIES
Tepoztlán	16[a]	66[b]	4[c]
Mitla	26[d]	89[b]	5[e]
Chan Kom	5	0	3
Soteapan	7	0	3

SOURCES: Redfield, *Tepoztlán*, pp. 48-49, 145-49, 153-55; Parsons, *Mitla*, pp. 42, 69; Redfield and Villa, *Chan Kom*, pp. 42, 69; and (for Soteapan) Foster, *A Primitive Mexican Economy*, pp. 19, 27-29.
[a] Included are storekeepers, teachers, butchers, shoemakers, carpenters, masons, ironworkers, bakers, barbers, herb doctors, midwives, fireworks makers, mask makers, magicians, corn merchants, and soft drink makers.
[b] Approximate figure.
[c] Includes mud-brick making, rope manufacture, belt weaving and bottling of soft drinks.
[d] Includes most of the occupations listed for Tepoztlán and also tanners, rope makers, charcoal burners, blacksmith, thatcher, carters, woodchoppers, weavers, tailors, brewers, candle makers, bandmasters, priest, image maker, and arti-ficial flavor maker.
[e] Includes liquor distilling, weaving, candle making, rope making, and mud-brick making. Mitla also had a mill for grinding corn.

bers shown by the table because a few individuals performed more than one specialized occupation and were counted more than once in arriving at the total figures. Furthermore, the great majority of these specialists also engaged in farming.

Redfield observed that in Tepoztlán there were some traditional nonagricultural occupations (magicians, for example) that were losing importance. In contrast to this, the introduction of new mechanical devices (such as the mill for grinding corn) gave increasing importance to more modern occupations. The new devices also brought with them technical specialists. As a rule these were individuals who had a more commercialized outlook on life. Mitla had more variety in its occupational structure, but as in Tepoztlán, its most specialized workers were aliens who had married local women. In the four villages women were mostly housewives, although there were some occupations, such as midwifery, which were performed by them exclusively.

The cottage industries were family undertakings in which each member performed a specific task. In most cases they had been practiced for many years and the equipment used, such as looms, was rather primitive. Some cottage industries, like the making of mud bricks, allowed a few individuals to make a living, but they were also practiced by any person needing the product for his own use; the raw materials were either freely provided by the environment or else they were easy to get from other persons in the village.

Compared to agriculture, the cottage industries and the other occupations played a much smaller role. They served to supplement earnings, but it does not seem that serious efforts were made to extend the marketing areas beyond the confines of the villages. Most families placed their main efforts on agriculture, only occasionally engaging in specialized activities.

In Chan Kom craft specialization was extremely limited and quite rudimentary, although some crafts, such as masonry and the making of candles, were known by all. In general, growing corn was the only way anyone made a living. In Soteapan something similar took place: there were a few individuals who occasionally obtained extra income from practicing a specialized craft, but they were all primarily agriculturalists. The cottage industries consisted of nothing more than the making of brown sugar, pots, or baskets—usually made when somebody needed them for personal use or consumption. For this reason table 7 shows some nonagricultural occupations and cottage industries but no employment outside agriculture.

All four villages were able to make local provision for most of their needs, but no village was self-sufficient; all of them participated actively in the interchange of goods with neighboring villages. To pay for their imports they used their surplus corn, poultry, fruits, and handicraft products. Tepoztlán and Mitla had stores that sold dry goods, drinks, canned foods, and the like. They also had marketplaces in which, once or twice a week, special market days were held. These attracted vendors and buyers from other villages, and since these days were rotated among a number of neighboring communities, there were merchants who traveled from one place to another until the circuit was completed. These traveling merchants were also a source of news; through them the villagers were able to keep informed of events in other places. Chan Kom and Soteapan had no market sites, but they had local stores and also received the visits of merchants who made regular trips to sell or barter.

In Mitla trade had an importance that was surpassed only by that of agriculture. Parsons saw Mitla as a business town whose life was permeated by price consciousness. Prices and money were of great interest to all, young and old, male and female, rich and poor alike. Everybody wanted to know the price of things, and money and costs entered into their everyday calculations. Parsons remarked of it: "The first of the valley towns to be reached from the mountain towns, Mitla is a natural middleman for trade, and a great many traders visit or pass through."[39] Most Mitla farmers, once the agricultural cycle was over and the dry season had arrived, became traveling merchants.[40] As a rule they banded in groups of two or three and traveled—on foot, horse, burro, or oxcart—to the mountain towns to purchase coffee, paying for it with various types of merchandise.[41]

Parsons explained that to buy one or more burros a man

39. Ibid., pp. 12, 60.
40. Ibid., p. 63. Parsons counted only seventy farmers who were not also traveling merchants.
41. Ibid., p. 14. Parsons reported once seeing a train of at least fifty burros bound for the coffee lands.

needed the savings of three or four years. If he lacked the
means to be an independent traveling merchant, he had the
choice of becoming an agent for a local store or for a merchant in Oaxaca, in which case he received some financial
backing from his principal.[42] Mitla had eight stores managed,
as a rule, by the women and children of the family. The
stores were important both because they provided extra income and because they were a mark of social distinction. In
contrast, the stores in Soteapan (there were about six of
them) were part-time enterprises. Here the people did not
show special interest in trade and rarely engaged in such
activities as the transport of goods.[43]

In all the villages, but especially in Mitla and Tepoztlán
there was extensive use of money. Barter had secondary importance. In Mitla most of it was of a ritual nature, that is,
associated with the performance of ancient customs. Chan
Kom and Soteapan had money economies, but in them barter
played a larger role. Sometimes barter took place among the
residents of the villages or else between them and the traveling merchants. In Chan Kom purchases involving large sums
of money were paid for in currency, but minor purchases
were usually paid with eggs or corn.[44] In Soteapan in 1941
the use of barter, while on the decline, was still quite prevalent. The coffee crop was almost always sold for money, but
there were certain commodities, such as lime, salt, or pots,
which were bartered for beans or corn.[45]

The two exchange systems did not always operate in con-
sistence with each other. In Soteapan at the time of Foster's
visit, salt was rarely sold for cash, but when it was the price
was 20 centavos a kilogram. On the other hand, a person was
able to trade on traditionally accepted terms a kilogram of
salt for a kilogram of beans; although the money price of the

---

42. Ibid., pp. 13-14.
43. Foster, *A Primitive Mexican Economy*, pp. 27, 47.
44. Redfield and Villa, *Chan Kom*, pp. 59-61.
45. Foster, *A Primitive Mexican Economy*, pp. 55-57.

latter was only 9 centavos. Another example is provided by the price of lime. In 1941 its money price was 11 centavos a kilogram, but in barter it exchanged for beans worth only 9 centavos. Five years before, at a time when beans were dear, a man could have done much better, because for his kilogram of lime, worth 11 centavos, he would have received a kilogram of beans, worth 18 centavos.

In some cases the barter exchange ratios fluctuated in response to changes in the money prices, but in other cases they were fixed and insensitive to money market conditions. Foster relates that vendors refused to sell their wares except for beans or corn and that laborers preferred to work for a fixed quantity of corn even though it may have been less than their wages had they chosen to be paid in money. He also relates that in years when the corn crop was poor and the price of corn was expected to rise there were no speculators even though some persons had both money and storage space and were not "adverse to turning a penny at the expense of their neighbors."[46]

These examples illustrate how money and barter existed side by side on quite incongruous terms: most of the time the money price of an article did not correspond to the money price of the article traded for it. The peasants themselves explained their actions by saying that "exchange is exchange," and thus it did not matter whether the price of beans, for example, was high or low.

Next to be examined is the land tenure system of the villages. In Mexico before 1910, land tenure was either private

46. Ibid., pp. 53-57. Charles Wagley in "Economics of a Guatemalan Village," *Memoirs of the American Anthropological Association,* no. 58, (1941), p. 22, witnessed something similar in the Guatemalan village of Santiago Chimaltenango in 1937. Traveling merchants came to the village quoting prices in corn and in money. The prices in corn remained unchanged for long periods of time despite the fact that the money price of corn in the city of Huehuetenango (only seventeen miles away) was subject to fluctuations. Many traveling merchants refused to sell their wares for money thus failing to adopt at the appropriate times the exchange system which would have led to the highest profit.

or communal. Communal tenure dates from pre-Columbian times and includes all the public lands held by municipal authorities. As mentioned previously, any of these lands can be used by a resident of a municipality, no matter where he lives. In practice, however, many villages consider nearby municipal lands as their own and use them exclusively. The revolution brought about land reform and with it a third type of tenure, the ejido.

When Chan Kom became a town in 1925 it was granted an ejido of 2,400 hectares. Since the number of agriculturalists was less than one hundred, they found themselves with an adequate supply of land. Not all the ejido was tillable, but most men farmed beyond its borders—mostly on land owned by the federal government.[47]

The other three villages, at least up to the time of the original village studies, had not been affected by the agrarian reform. Soteapan, like Chan Kom, did not seem to have a land problem, and except for the houses and their lots, which were privately owned, all the other lands were communal. A man wanting to farm claimed unoccupied land. Fallow lands held in reserve occasionally led to disputes, particularly when trees had been planted on them because trees, unlike land, were subject to private property. Land near the village was harder to get than land farther away, but except for this inconvenience, land was otherwise plentiful. It is of interest to note that although land could be had for the taking most men limited their claims to plots of from less than one hectare to two hectares, the size that their agricultural techniques allowed them to cultivate.

In Mitla land tenure was both private and communal. Parsons found that out of 446 households, 244 were landless, that is, they did not own private land. On the other hand there was a small group of men with large private holdings, some of which were acquired through defaulted mortgage

47. Redfield and Villa, *Chan Kom*, pp. 64-65.

loans made at high rates of interest.[48] Some of these wealthy
men had made attempts to irrigate their lands and had also
introduced new crops such as chick-peas and alfalfa. Since
some peasants seemingly owned small private plots while
others had the choice of becoming sharecroppers in the
hacienda, Parsons was led to believe that there was no land
hunger in Mitla.

Redfield got a similar impression in Tepoztlán. He wrote:
"Not only does Tepoztlán maintain itself almost entirely by
farming, but nearly every Tepoztecan is a farmer. Most families have at least a small *milpa*. . . ."[49] The milpas, according
to him, provided work for all the men in the village.[50] In
contrast to this assessment, Lewis, writing about conditions
in 1944, observed that 80 percent of the municipal lands
(these being the communal lands) were, for the most part,
unfit for agriculture. The other 20 percent constituted the
tillable land, 5 percent being ejido and 15 percent being
private land. He noted that out of a total of 853 families, 202
owned private land only; 158 owned ejido land only; 109
owned private land and ejido; and 384 (45 percent) owned
neither ejido nor private land.[51] He doubted whether the
situation had been any better in 1926–27, because in the
intervening years ejidos had been granted to 267 families,
158 of which had previously been landless.[52] Apart from this,

48. Parsons, *Mitla,* p. 54. Parsons reports that one of these wealthy men
owned a hacienda in which more than 200 tenants worked on a half-share
basis. He also owned, among other things, a Rolls-Royce.
49. Redfield, *Tepoztlán,* p. 145. A *milpa* is a small plot where corn is grown
by primitive methods.
50. Ibid., p. 122.
51. O. Lewis, *Life in a Mexican Village,* table 25, p. 123.
52. Of course even without private land or ejido a man still had the opportunity to do a limited amount of farming on the communal lands. Redfield
counted 714 houses in Tepoztlán at the time of his study. It is not made
clear whether all the houses were occupied, but on the other hand in
some houses more than one household unit may have lived and thus Redfield's count may be taken as the approximate number of households in
the village. Using the population figure given by table 3 for 1930 it can be
found that the average household unit in the village consisted of 3.6 persons.
If this figure be taken as average for the entire municipality of Tepoztlán, it

he found that the size of both the private and the ejido holdings was too small—a situation resulting from the tillable land being in short supply rather than from a lopsided land distribution. According to him, 90.6 percent of all private holdings were less than nine hectares and 68.4 percent were less than four hectares. There were many small holdings, some as small as one-fifth of a hectare, and there were only six

TABLE 8

Agricultural Characteristics of the Villages, 1930

VILLAGE	CULTURE	NUMBER OF MAIN CROPS	MAIN TOOLS	NONHUMAN SOURCES OF POWER
Tepoztlán	Plow, hoe[a]	2	Plow, stick	Oxen
Mitla	Plow	2	Plow	Oxen
Chan Kom	Hoe	1	Stick	None
Soteapan	Hoe	3	Stick	None

SOURCE: Data from the original village studies (passim).
[a] Plow culture involves the use of plow and oxen; hoe culture involves the use of slash-and-burn techniques.

holdings of from twenty to twenty-nine hectares.[53] As far as the ejido holdings were concerned, they were less than three hectares in size, 95.9 percent of them consisting of less than two hectares.[54] Considering the small size of the holdings (of all types) and the number of landless families, there is little doubt that Tepoztlán faced land scarcity in 1944. Whether in 1926–27 the situation was less serious cannot be determined conclusively because, among other things, the population was much smaller.

Additional aspects of the agricultural situation of the villages are presented in table 8. As in the nation at large, in all

probably had around 1,300 household units. Taking 20 percent of the municipal land as tillable it can be found that the average amount of tillable land per household unit in the municipality was 5.3 hectares. Normally, and with allowance for the agricultural methods used, this amount of land should have been adequate to support a family of less than four persons.
53. O. Lewis, *Life in a Mexican Village,* table 21, p. 120.
54. Ibid., table 24, p. 123.

four villages corn was the number one crop. Beans were another important crop in three villages, and coffee was a third important crop in one village. Tepoztlán was the only community where two argicultural methods were practiced; one was plow culture, the other was hoe or slash-and-burn culture. Plow culture was practiced on both private and ejido lands. The plow-oxen combination was the one usually employed since it allowed planting from one year to the next. Two types of plows were used, one made of steel and one made of wood. The latter was made locally and being cheaper it was also the most popular.

Hoe culture was practiced on communal lands, mainly by those to whom no other land was available. It involved the burning and clearing of small tracts on steep mountain slopes. On these tracts corn was planted with the aid of a digging stick and other primitive tools. These plots were cultivated one or two years; after this time their fertility was exhausted and they had to be left fallow.

Both hoe culture and plow culture depended on seasonal rain, and both produced one crop a year. Data on yields are not available, but it is generally known that the productivity of hoe culture, at least during the year of burning, is greater than that of plow culture. In Tepoztlán this seems to have occurred, as data provided by Lewis show.[55]

Beans were the second most important crop in Tepoztlán's agriculture. They were planted, sometimes with corn, in the fields and frequently in the backyards of the houses. Also grown, usually in small quantities, were vegetables (such as squash, tomatoes, coffee, and chick-peas) and a number of fruit trees (orange, banana, lime, lemon, hog plum, and others). Detailed information concerning the size of all these crops is lacking, but it seems that Tepoztlán produced the great bulk of its food.[56]

55. Ibid., p. 130.
56. Stuart Chase, *Mexico: A Study of Two Americas* (New York: Macmillan Co., 1931), p. 214.

In Mitla only plow culture was practiced. Most of the plows used were wooden, but some of the most prosperous farmers owned American plows.[57] Planting was done by hand and foot with the aid of primitive tools. Again corn and beans were the main crops, but the Mitla farmers also raised the following crops: castor-oil plant, alfalfa, bamboo, chick-peas, century plant (used to make liquor and rope), and two types of cactus (one used to make fences and another used as fodder). One man also raised wheat.

Parsons noticed in Mitla particular deficiencies (which, incidentally, were common to all four villages): there was no rotation of crops, no use of fertilizers, no attempt to remove stones from the fields, and practically no irrigation. Hence she stated that the peasants of Mitla appeared to be indifferent farmers.[58]

There is no detailed account of what the farmers of the four villages did to improve their productive facilities. It may be true that in some cases they did not bother to improve their land, but it is also true that some of them bought oxen, horses, burros, steel and wooden plows, oxcarts, etc. Others built granaries, and some were even able to start small commercial establishments. The expenditures on all these items were capital investments, and at least to this extent the farmers were not indifferent. An additional factor should be taken into account: the responsiveness of the peasants depended in good measure on the migratory nature of agriculture. Every one or two years different plots had to be cultivated; so the momentary attachment to a particular piece of land was not

57. Parsons, *Mitla*, p. 52. Wooden plows were cheaper, but of course they could not cut into the soil as deeply as steel plows. The lower price of the former may have been one reason why farmers preferred them but it was not the only one. The terrain around Mitla is in some places so full of rocks (some of which look more like boulders) that the steel plows were easily broken and did not last as long as the wooden ones. It may be added that in Tepoztlán the hills on which hoe culture was practiced were so steep and rocky that they also forced farmers into the use of primitive tools. It would have been impossible to use plow and oxen on these slopes.
58. Ibid., p. 53.

conducive to improvements of a long-term nature. Nevertheless, improvements were still undertaken. Foster relates that in Soteapan in 1935 a group of about thirty men banded together to erect a barbed wire fence around their corn plots in order to protect them from roving pigs and other animals.[59] Thus it seems that, whether collective or individual, a certain amount of investment took place in the villages.

Only one type of agriculture was practiced in Soteapan: hoe culture. It exhausted the fertility of the soil in from five to ten years, and this meant that the plots had to remain fallow for a similar period. The three main crops were corn, beans, and coffee. In contrast to Mitla and Tepoztlán, which both cultivated one crop per year, two crops were the rule in Soteapan. Corn was grown mainly to satisfy local consumption; beans were the principal cash crop, and as mentioned before, large quantities of them were bartered to merchants.[60] The third main crop was coffee. Its cultivation had been known since before the turn of the century, but production in large scale started only after the revolution. Foster explains that no special trees were grown to shade the coffee trees but that there were wooded areas that served the same purpose. He also relates that young trees were cheap and that the growing of coffee was the most profitable local activity.[61] Profits, however, seem to have exerted little influence because corn never lost its supremacy. Though limited, coffee production exceeded local needs and the surplus was exported. Hogs were another export item; so the people of Soteapan had beans, coffee, and hogs to pay for the commodities that came from the outside. They also grew other vegetables (squash, small onions, root crops, etc.), sugar cane (from which brown sugar and syrup were obtained), a number of fruits (mainly bananas, pineapple, mango, papaya), and herbs and spices.

59. Foster, *A Primitive Mexican Economy*, p. 81.
60. Ibid., p. 54.
61. Ibid., p. 84.

Unlike Mitla, Soteapan did not have extreme differences
in the distribution of wealth. Some villagers were better off
than others, mainly because they worked harder or showed
more initiative, but the differences were small. Foster relates
the case of a man who had become wealthy by engaging in
activities that included building an oven and baking bread,
operating a small store, using a sewing machine to make
pants, planting rice, and experimenting with a plow. He
used the latter on what appeared to be an exhausted piece
of land and obtained a good crop.[62]

Hoe culture prevailed in Chan Kom where the most important crop was also corn. Only a few men planted other
crops, but these included beans, sweet potatoes, squash, peppers, some root crops, and some fruits. The use of slash-and-
burn agriculture meant that land was cultivated for two suc-
cessive years after which it was left to rest for seven years.
This system, needless to say, posed stringent requirements.
Under the 2 to 7 ratio indicated, for every plot under cultivation it was necessary to have in reserve, as a minimum, three
and a half plots of similar size. Fortunately for Chan Kom,
this presented no problem, because with a small population,
its supply of land was more than adequate to meet its needs.[63]

It may seem at this point that Chan Kom's agricultural
system rested on a wasteful use of land. This is only partly
true. The Yucatecan peasant, living in a peninsula which is
a shelf of porous limestone with shallow patches of soil, has
no better system available. Steggerda explained this as follows: "The shallowness of the soil does not permit the use of

62. Ibid., p. 89.
63. Morris Steggerda. *Maya Indians of Yucatán*, Carnegie Institution Publication No. 531 (Washington, 1941), pp. 114, 149. Steggerda states that in the
thirties in the state of Yucatán the ratio of land in use to land left fallow
was 2 to 10. Under this ratio a peasant required six fields of similar size:
one in actual use and five fallow. Taking this into account he explains that
according to his calculations the land was capable of supporting eight times
as many people as there were at that time. Angel Palerm in his "Agricultural
Systems and Food Patterns," (in *Social Anthropology*, vol. 6, ed. Manning
Nash [Austin: University of Texas Press, 1967], p. 32) mentions an average
ratio of 1 to 8 for Mesoamerica.

modern farming implements. The only tools used in a Yucatán cornfield are a machete, an ax, and a planting stick. . . . In modern times there is sufficient land to allow the field to revert to bush after two or three years of cultivation, and consequently turning sod is not a necessary agricultural practice."[64] However primitive the agricultural system may have been, in 1931 the average amount of corn produced per family was more than twice the amount required to meet consumption needs, and thus a surplus was available to exchange for other goods.

In all the villages corn was the principal component of the diet but not the only one.[65] Most families raised chickens or turkeys; some also raised pigs and cattle. These animals either supplemented the diet or were exchanged for other goods. In addition most families ate beans and chili peppers, and occasionally rice, canned food, and bread. Milk in Mitla and Chan Kom was rarely drunk because people did not like it. What they seemed to enjoy for meals was a number of vegetables, fruits, wild game, wild plants and roots, and in the case of Soteapan, fish. Some families kept bees, from which they obtained wax—used to make candles—and honey, which became part of the diet. In general, the villagers were more or less well fed. Foster remarked that in Soteapan the food seemed to be adequate, that people appeared healthy, and that real famine was unknown—even in 1941, a year in which the corn crop was poor.[66] Commenting about the people of Yucatán and Tepoztlán, Chase wrote: "Nobody is ever seriously hungry; famines are unknown. Stomach-ache is the

---

64. Steggerda, *Maya Indians,* pp. 90-92. Augusto Pérez Toro in "La agricultura milpera de los mayas de Yucatán," *Enciclopedia yucatense,* vol. 6 (Mexico, 1946), p. 173, concurs with Steggerda's view when he states that the nature of the soil does not allow radical innovations in agricultural techniques.

65. Ibid., p. 89. Steggerda estimated that corn comprised from 70 to 80 percent of the diet of the Yucatecan peasant. Foster (*A Primitive Mexican Economy,* p. 63) estimated that 80 percent of all food consumed by the people of Soteapan was corn. Toro ("La agricultura milpera," p. 200) attributes the preeminence given corn by the Maya to its being their most important food.

66. Foster, *A Primitive Mexican Economy,* p. 63.

ranking disease."[67] Furthermore, in all the villages there were numerous feasts and social celebrations during which large quantities of food were consumed.[68]

In the four villages there were persons who owned pack animals and a few who owned oxen. In Mitla there were several families that owned small flocks of sheep and goats. There were no areas used exclusively for grazing; instead, the animals were allowed to roam and feed in the open fields. No effort was made to properly care for them, although at times they were rounded up and fed corn and corn husks and stalks.

The forest or, in the case of Chan Kom, the bush provided many useful products in addition to fodder, for instance, medicinal herbs (which were important because none of the villages had a doctor),[69] firewood, and materials for house construction (such as poles, beams, thatch, clay, lime, vines, etc.). The construction of a house required a limited amount of these materials. Mud bricks, wattle and daub, or masonry (in a few cases) were used for the walls. For the roof, thatch was most frequently used, although in Mitla and Tepoztlán there was a tendency toward the use of tiles. The floors were usually made of dirt, and except for some houses of the well-to-do, the majority had neither windows, glass fixtures, nor stovepipes. Most houses had a section set aside for crop storage, and others had separate granaries. At times fowl

67. Chase, *Mexico*, p. 131.
68. Steggerda, *Maya Indians*, p. 74, notes that the Mayas' "total energy intake averaged 2,565 calories, which is low when compared with the daily energy intake (3,500 calories) of the average American laborer." However, he also confirmed the findings of earlier investigations that showed the basal metabolism of the Maya to be 8 percent higher (indicating a more efficient heat production) than the standards for white men of the same weight, age, and height. These findings are also discussed in F. G. Benedict and M. Steggerda, *The Food of the Present-Day Maya Indians of Yucatán*, Carnegie Institution Publication No. 456, (Washington, D. C., 1937), pp. 157-58.
69. The only exception was Tepoztlán where, according to Redfield (*Tepoztlán*, pp. 166-67), a Bulgarian doctor took up residence in 1925 or 1926. However, since many people continued to go to the herbalists, he was unsuccessful in his practice and soon left the village.

houses were also built, and many houses had backyards with special areas reserved for burros, cows, or pigs. Finally, all properties included a plot of land which sometimes was planted with fruit trees or vegetables.

The house furnishings were mainly pre-Columbian and sometimes simply consisted of various utensils needed for the preparation of food. Tables, chairs, and beds were rarely found in the poorer houses. In Soteapan and Chan Kom hammocks were commonly used for sleeping. In Mitla and Tepoztlán people slept on straw mats on the floor or on primitive beds made of bamboo sticks. A few families owned china dishes, drinking glasses, metal pans, beds, etc. One modern piece of equipment had found its way into the homes of poor and rich alike (except perhaps in Chan Kom) —and that was the sewing machine.[70] These machines were constantly used by many families to make garments either for themselves or for others, even though at times ready-made clothing was also purchased.[71]

The clothing consisted of a combination of Spanish and Indian garments. The textiles were occasionally made locally on primitive looms, but for the most part they were factory-made. Most of the time people either went barefoot or wore sandals. On Sundays or special occasions, shoes were sometimes worn, and women also wore embroidered dresses and gold jewelry. To protect themselves from the rain, both men and women sometimes wore capes made of shredded palm. Straw hats were usually worn by the men.

Clothing can be used to illustrate how contact with the outside affected the economic activities of the villages. In Soteapan before the revolution, there had been an emphasis on the production of a variety of homemade goods. These included pottery, baskets, clothing, sandals, and hats. After

---

70. Tannenbaum, "Technology and Race in Mexico," p. 378, also noted the popularity of the sewing machine. He found that 90.5 percent of the villages sampled had one.

71. Foster, *A Primitive Mexican Economy*, p. 47, n. 2, notes that in Soteapan sewing machines were bought on installments. The village had seven of them.

the revolution, linked to the growing importance of coffee production, a tendency toward the purchase of ready-made goods developed, and the old arts and crafts began to disappear.[72] The same thing happened in Tepoztlán. In the old days some garments were made in the village on ancient looms, but when Redfield was there all textiles were "imported either as ready-made garments or as cloth to make up into clothing, except some of the women's belts which were still made locally."[73]

Parsons believed that some primitive goods continued in use because they were cheaper as when, for instance, a man lived under thatch because he could not afford a tile roof. When the innovation was cheaper—a woman's cotton dress against a woolen one—it was quickly substituted, provided it did not interfere too much with the old habits. In other cases people refrained from buying such things as beds or sandals not because they could not afford them but because they were used to doing without them.[74]

In regard to the distribution of wealth, it may be noted that Soteapan and Chan Kom constituted egalitarian societies. In them persons could be found who were wealthier than others, but wealth was fluid and extreme differences between rich and poor were unknown. Besides, various usages worked toward equality. All the people considered themselves Indian and spoke the native language; they dressed alike and enjoyed the same type of housing, food, clothing, and other material possessions. Tepoztlán and Mitla, on the other hand,

72. Ibid., pp. 29, 51.
73. R. Redfield, *Tepoztlán*, p. 46. Erland Nordenskiöld observed something similar in two South American tribes. See *The Changes in the Material Culture of Two Indian Tribes under the Influence of New Surroundings*, Comparative Ethnographical Studies, no. 2 (Göteborg 1920), p. 201. He wrote, "The negative influence of the Whites has of course been very great here. The primitive tools have disappeared, a number of implements and ornaments have become rare or have vanished, a quantity of domestic industry has become superfluous, since readymade things have been purchasable from the Whites. The Indian domestic industry is gradually disappearing, but is not transformed under the influence of the Whites."
74. Parsons, *Mitla*, pp. 531-32.

had a small group of individuals that constituted a separate class. They were richer and better educated; they had more modern homes and clothes and had traveled to the city; they had more influence in the affairs of the village and were responsible for the introduction of a number of innovations. In the case of Mitla reference has already been made to one member of this group who owned a hacienda, but there were others even wealthier. For instance, a contemporary of his owned two large houses, two stores, two ranches, forty teams of oxen, a herd of about twenty steers, several pieces of land, the corn mill (which also supplied electricity for the public lighting in the center of the village and for some fifteen households that were able to afford it), a motor truck, and a cinema—which he introduced. In addition this man had been municipal president twice and had been the first one to make irrigation ditches and to plant alfalfa. Some of these men, in the process of acquiring wealth for themselves tried to improve the condition of their villages. Often, when not engaged in new undertakings, they performed a variety of public and social services and consequently were a source of social betterment to the entire village.

A second effective source of social betterment was the pre-Columbian practice of communal labor. This type of labor was performed by all the adult males for the public good and involved no remuneration. Communal labor opened trails, built schools, and ran the village governments. It was a duty to be performed, and failure to comply meant fines or even imprisonment. Furthermore, for some public works a man was expected to contribute not only labor but also materials or money. In Mitla (with the exception of the municipal secretary who was paid) and in Chan Kom, all the officials in charge of the public administration served without pay. This placed certain hardships on the persons holding offices so the offices were rotated according to various rules, but in one capacity or another all men performed public services. Communal labor was also used for the organization and support of various religious celebrations. In Mitla and Tepoztlán some lands were worked communally for the sole purpose of defraying religious expenditures. Some communal labor was also used for private tasks, especially for the construction of houses. In Chan Kom and Soteapan, in particular, houses were usually built with the cooperation of relatives and neighbors. When a man received this type of assistance, he was of course expected to reciprocate when called upon.

Musicians, town officials, and sacristans were exempt from both communal labor and from the payment of taxes. The latter were small and placed no heavy burden on those who had to pay them, but in spite of this, they were frequently resented. In Mitla all the males over fifteen years of age had to pay a monthly school tax of 24 centavos. There was also a state tax of 1 percent assessed on houses and land, and stores paid a monthly state tax of around 12 pesos.[75]

In Soteapan the stores paid a tax of 1 peso a month, the fee for recording births and deaths was 40 centavos, and for each cow killed within the municipality a fee of 5 pesos was charged. The biggest taxpayer was the government-owned petroleum company which had some unworked deposits in the municipality. A hydro-electric plant located several miles away paid only a token tax, but it furnished power to some twenty street lights and to one private subscriber.[76] Fines were an additional source of revenue. All told, Foster estimated that the municipality operated on a budget of around 2,000 pesos a year.

In Tepoztlán there were four taxes: on real estate, on the sale of domestic animals, on the use of the slaughterhouse, and on merchants using the market place.[77] Redfield observed that the municipal government was unable to initiate public improvements because its revenues were inadequate and one reason for this was that the valuation of property was in the

75. Ibid., pp. 162-63.
76. Foster, *A Primitive Mexican Economy*, pp. 72-73.
77. Redfield, *Tepoztlán*, pp. 66-67.

hands of a group of individuals who set low assessments on
their lands and on those of their neighbors.

With these brief comments about the various taxes the
discussion of the base period is now almost complete. Only
one more aspect of village life remains to be considered, the
production-consumption-expenditure pattern of some households. The case of a Soteapan household that can be considered typical is examined first. With data provided by
Foster[78] the following facts can be established: the household
consisted of four persons and the amount of land cultivated
was 1.9 hectares. The agricultural year 1940–41 was quite
poor owing to drought, and consequently production (especially of corn) was below normal. However, if an average is
taken for the years 1936–39, it can be roughly estimated that
the annual corn production of the family was around 3,000
kilograms. The production of beans came to around 400 kilograms. This was actually the 1942 production, which was also
considered to be below normal. Finally, the production of
coffee amounted to around 172 kilograms. Taking these three
products as the main sources of income and using the prices
then prevailing (1941), it can be estimated that the value
of the output of these three crops amounted to 311.75 pesos.[79]
The value of the portion consumed by the family (including
corn fed to animals and corn used to pay hired labor)
amounted to 137.25 pesos. Other miscellaneous expenditures
(including wearing apparel in the amount of 107.25 pesos
and other items such as soap, sugar, pots, cooking utensils,
etc.) amounted to 156.85 pesos.[80] This left a balance of 17.65
pesos, but in addition the family would have contributed
35 pesos to the church (in the form of some corn and perhaps
a pig), and social consumption (including the value of the

78. Foster, *A Primitive Mexican Economy*, pp. 21-23 and chap. 5.
79. The exchange rate between the dollar and the Mexican peso at the time
of the original village studies was (in pesos to the dollar): 1926, 2.07; 1927-30,
2.12; 1931, 2.43; 1941, 4.85. Since 1954 it has been 12.50 pesos to the dollar.
80. Expenditures were curtailed in bad years, so it is not definite whether
after a poor harvest the family would have expended the sum indicated.

animals slaughtered, produce consumed, etc.) would have required another 16 pesos. Hence, this particular year this family would have had a deficit of 33.35 pesos.

It must be pointed out that this is of course a hypothetical deficit. Sources of income other than the three main crops have been ignored even though they would have included such important items as the output of fruits, pork, poultry, and eggs. Then, since 1941 was a poor year, it is likely that some voluntary contributions or some expenditures would not have been incurred. In short, whereas the income has been understated owing to lack of data, the expenditures may have been overstated, and rather than a deficit a surplus may have been the net result.

With data provided by Redfield, Villa, and Steggerda it is possible to make an approximate estimate of the production and consumption of the average family in Chan Kom.[81] On the basis of a five year average (1933–37), Steggerda determined that a family consisting of five persons produced 2,982 kilograms of corn per year. The amount consumed was 1,596 kilograms (including corn fed to animals which amounted to around one-third of the total amount consumed). At the price prevalent at the time (3.50 pesos for 42 kilograms), the value of the corn produced came to 248.50 pesos, and the value of the corn consumed came to 133 pesos. Thus there was a surplus of 115.50 pesos. A middle income family consisting of a man, his wife, and two small children would have had expenditures of 100.70 pesos (including 69.90 pesos for wearing apparel and expenditures on other items such as meat, salt, sugar, coffee, gunpowder, spices, perfume, candles, etc.). This would have left him with 14.80 pesos available for other expenditures or savings. Again, as in the previous example, income from sources other than the main crop has been omitted, and therefore the total income has been understated.

---

81. The data on family corn production are taken from Steggerda, *Maya Indians,* pp. 124-27; the data on consumption are taken from Redfield and Villa, *Chan Kom,* pp. 56-57.

The awareness of the peasants concerning prices and their responsiveness to prices impressed Redfield in the same way that similar traits had impressed Parsons in Mitla.[82] Redfield observed that the production of corn was influenced not only by consumption needs but by the prevailing price (in this case mainly by the price at the city of Valladolid, which was the market where most peasants sold their corn).[83] To illustrate this price awareness and responsiveness it may be pointed out that in 1930 the price of corn fell, with the result that the following year the area under cultivation was reduced by almost one-third,[84] in the expectation perhaps of similar low prices. After the 1930 harvest the surplus corn, rather than being sold, was kept in reserve for family consumption in anticipation of the reduced 1931 crop.[85]

In addition to low prices, weather could also spell the difference between a good and a bad crop. In this respect not only did the peasant have to reckon with too much or too little rainfall, he also had to select accurately the time for burning. If he burned too soon, the still damp bush would not burn well; if he waited too long, the rains could prevent burning entirely. Then, he had to contend with insects, birds, rodents, and other marauding animals that ate a share of the crop.[86] To protect himself against them, he had devised various ingenious practices, but these were in many cases rather primitive and not altogether effective. These conditions were not restricted to Chan Kom but existed in the other three villages as well.

No detailed data on production and consumption are avail-

---

82. See p. 39.
83. Redfield and Villa, *Chan Kom,* pp. 51-52.
84. The price of 42 kg. of shelled corn could fluctuate from 1 to 9 pesos. In the other three villages the fluctuations of corn prices were equally severe.
85. Under the circumstances the peasants' consumption would probably have remained at the same level although their overall purchasing ability would have been impaired.
86. Steggerda, *Maya Indians,* p. 135. This author mentions that in Yucatán between 1535 and 1835, at average intervals of 19.8 years, there were fifteen great famines caused by lack of rain, floods, hurricanes, or plagues of grasshoppers.

able for families of Mitla and Tepoztlán. But what has been said about the households of the other two villages indicates that in a normal year, in spite of the heavy odds set by the hostility of the environment or by low prices, the average family could meet its consumption needs and actual expenditures out of the income provided by the main crops so that the income from secondary sources could have gone into special expenditures or into savings.

There is indirect evidence which shows that savings were probably rather large. It includes the accumulation of family wealth, such as masonry houses, cattle, or jewelry,[87] and also the considerable number of public and private festivals, most of which involved heavy expenditures. In Soteapan there were various special occasions that required the preparation of large quantities of food.[88] A funeral, for instance, required one or more pigs, a number of chickens, liquor, corn, beans, coffee, chocolate, and even more. This food was offered to visitors and musicians at the time of the funeral and then at another celebration that was held two or three weeks later. The cost of one of these funerals could run from 30 pesos to around 60 pesos or more. In some cases friends contributed some of the food, but it seems that such contributions had to be repaid at a later date. Then there were other events, such as the honoring of particular saints, that required similar expenditures.

House building was also an occasion for feasting. On an assigned day a man usually enlisted the help of some fifteen friends, but in return he had to spend about 30 pesos to feed them properly. Most of the time the house was not completed in one day so that a second get-together was required—

87. Redfield and Villa, *Chan Kom*, p. 58, report that savings went into masonry houses, tools, household furnishings, cattle, and women's gold chains. They add: "Some men store up savings in the form of money, usually buried in some part of the house lot. Or, if piety or desire for conspicuous leadership takes hold of a man, he may become the sponsor of a local fiesta in honor of a *santo*, and spend all his year's savings at one stroke."
88. Foster, *A Primitive Mexican Economy*, pp. 30-38, 64-70.

usually the following year. Foster thought that houses could have been built more efficiently by the use of hired labor, but this would have run counter to tradition and no man followed such a course.

Weddings were also expensive affairs, although in many instances couples simply started living together as man and wife. The two major religious feasts were also costly celebrations, and their preparation required the labor of many men and women for several days. Foster estimated the cost of one of them (including expenditures on food, music, religious services, etc.) at more than 500 pesos. To meet the costs of these feasts the people made contributions in money or in kind, the largest contribution coming from the man honored as mayordomo of the feast.

Chan Kom also had a number of festal occasions, some which were of Christian origin and some which were pagan rituals associated with several agricultural practices and with the honoring of pagan gods. An important part of these cere-monies, which required the participation of many persons, was the preparation and consumption of considerable quan-tities of special food and drink. There were also the usual private feasts. Marriage, in particular, involved the perform-ance of a number of traditional practices that required large expenditures on the part of the bridegroom and his family.[89]

Tepoztlán had close to thirty important feasts of various kinds; some were national (such as independence day), some affected the whole village (such as the carnival), some were restricted to one of the seven chapels of the village. In addi-tion there were feasts in other communities which were

---

89. Redfield and Villa, *Chan Kom*, pp. 192-98, indicate that besides gifts of rum, cigarettes, chocolate, and bread, which were presented on behalf of the bridegroom to the prospective bride's family on various occasions, the wed-ding gift itself ordinarily included "a gold chain 'of two loops,' two rings of specified quality, two hair ribbons, one silk handkerchief, several meters of cotton cloth, two or three silver pesos, rum, bread, chocolate and cigarettes." Later, the bride was also given a long dress of fine cloth and a shawl. Finally, there was the wedding itself which involved many expenditures, usually taken care of by the father of the bridegroom.

attended by many Tepoztecans. The duration of these feasts varied; some required only one day, but others required as long as a week and involved the preparation of fireworks, cockfights, dances, and rustic bullfights. Needless to say, all these celebrations were rather costly. A man participating in a secular feast, such as the carnival, had to meet three costs: a contribution to a general carnival fund, the abandonment of his work for several days, and the purchase of an expensive costume of silk or velvet.

Mitla also had numerous feasts. Those of an important religious nature alone numbered twenty-one.[90] In this village, as in Tepoztlán, the income from special communal lands was used to defray part of the costs. Another part was paid by the mayordomo in charge of the feast. This part, however, involved such heavy expenditures that the office of mayordomo had to be rotated each year. Among other duties a mayordomo had to make arrangements for the religious ceremonies and supply candles, food, drink, and tobacco for the musicians as well as for all those who visited his home during the time of the feast. Some people helped the mayordomo with chickens, turkeys, eggs, liquor, and other goods, but these contributions were carefully recorded and sooner or later had to be repaid. The case of mayordomos ending their tour of duty in debt was not uncommon. If a mayordomo died in debt his obligation was not wiped out but was taken over by the surviving members of his family. During his adult life a man was expected to be mayordomo at least twice.

Special arrangements were made in the case of the principal feast. To help defray its costs people were taxed small sums for various specific purposes: to buy liquor, to pay for games, to rent the cinema, and so on. Bullfights were a popular part of the feast, and the bulls for them were usually loaned by the owners. Finally, affairs such as funerals and weddings were also expensive. The cost of a wedding, for

90. Parsons, *Mitla,* p. 192.

instance, ran between 200 and 600 pesos. Of course not everybody spent such a large sum; many poor people limited the
cost of a wedding to around 50 pesos.

It is obvious that all the festivities mentioned had a social
and cultural meaning. In the scheme of values of the village
peasants, such festivities had a justified place, and their social
or cultural value took precedence over their monetary costs.
What should be noted, however, is that the villages had the
necessary means for meeting the expenditures associated with
them and that feasts, in fact, were one important outlet for
savings.

This brings to an end the discussion of the base period. It
may simply be added that the account given thus far, while
providing a point of departure from which to trace the progress of the villages, does not of course compare with the
works of the scholars who first studied them. In their works
the reader will find a richness of detail that has here been
put aside. The villages themselves, while presenting many
common traits, nevertheless have characteristics that give
them individual personalities. As Tannenbaum remarked,
"Each Mexican community has a personality of its own, and
only a great artist could do proper justice to it."[91]

91. Tannenbaum, "Technology and Race in Mexico," p. 366.

3

Three Decades of Rural Progress

The account given in the previous chapter covers the most important aspects of the economic life of the villages in the early thirties. This chapter and the following two examine the changes that occurred between the time of the original studies and the time of the author's survey of the villages in the spring of 1964. The period under review spans some thirty-seven years in the case of Tepoztlán, thirty-three years in the case of Mitla and Chan Kom, and twenty-three years in the case of Soteapan.

Examining the national picture first, there can be little question that between 1930 and 1960 Mexico posted a remarkable record of economic progress. The thirties were the years that signaled the beginning of Mexico's modern growth. It was during these years that the country broke with its traditional past. With the revolution and the years of turmoil behind, it was as though the country had made up its mind to catch up with the twentieth century.

This does not wrest importance from the preceding decade, because the twenties established the groundwork for much of the progress that came after. During the twenties several programs designed to promote the long-run development of the country were initiated. Mention has already been made of the agrarian reform,[1] but infrastructural and other public

1. In the opinion of many persons the agrarian reform was the main achievement of the revolution, first, because it did away with a feudalistic land tenure system, and second, because it became the prime generator of Mexico's later growth. One of the most important programs undertaken

investments also received attention. In 1925, for example, the central bank was established; in 1926 the irrigation and road construction programs began and the first national bank for agricultural credit was inaugurated.

For purposes of the present study it seems unnecessary to trace in laborious detail the economic development of Mexico from the thirties to the early sixties.[2] A few salient achievements, however, will help set the national stage before the spotlight is thrown again on the villages. In these three decades the length of the road network increased thirteen-fold, annual oil production went up from 38 million barrels to 126 million barrels, the generation of electrical energy advanced tenfold, and industrial production increased its share of GNP from 14 percent to 24 percent.[3] In 1934 only 149 thousand hectares were under irrigation; by the middle of 1964 the figure had climbed to 3 million hectares.[4] The output of cotton registered a tenfold advance; that of coffee and corn moved up more than threefold; that of wheat, fivefold. The value of imports posted an increase from 93 to 1,240 million dollars and that of exports from 179 to 931 million dollars. Mexico became popular with American tourists, and as

under the agrarian reform was land redistribution. It started in 1917 and has continued up to the present time.

2. The economic development of the last decades has been the subject of many studies. Among them are the following: International Bank for Reconstruction and Development, *The Economic Development of Mexico* (Baltimore: Johns Hopkins Press, 1953); Raymond Vernon, *The Dilemma of Mexico's Development* (Cambridge: Harvard University Press, 1963); V. F. Bravo, *Mexico y su desarrollo económico* (Mexico, 1963); Adolf Sturmthal, "Economic Development, Income Distribution and Capital Formation in Mexico," *Journal of Political Economy* (June 1955), p. 183; D. H. Shelton, "Mexico's Economic Growth: Success of Diversified Development," *Southwestern Social Science Quarterly* 41, no. 3 (December 1960): p. 304; Alfredo Navarrete, Jr., "Mexico's Economic Growth: Prospects and Problems," in *Economic Growth,* ed. Eastin Nelson (Austin: University of Texas Press, 1960), p. 127. Other studies can be found in Alfonso Ayensa, *Bioliografía industrial de Mexico, 1962* (Mexico: Banco de Mexico, 1962.)

3. These and the following data are from Antonio Ortiz Mena, "XXX Aniversario de nacional financiera, 1934-1964," *El mercado de valores* (Mexico) 6 July 1964, p. 381. All Changes mentioned apply to the 1934-64 period.

4. This figure represents 20 percent of the land under cultivation in 1964. In 1930 the land under cultivation amounted to 7.1 million ha.

a result income from tourism jumped from 30 to 655 million dollars, thus allowing the central bank to expand its monetary reserves from 29 to 524 million dollars. GNP (in 1950 prices) reflected all these forward moves, and thus it rose from 15,927 million pesos to 84,700 million pesos. Of course the population of the country also leaped forward; by mid-1964 it was around 40 million. Interestingly enough, average income per capita (in real terms) not only withstood the population rise but followed suit; it more than doubled. Then, while the rural population decreased to 49 percent, the illiterate population shrank to 38 percent.[5]

These figures give an idea of the remarkable and diversified growth of the country during the three decades under consideration. The question is, how did the four villages fare while the nation at large was setting such records? To answer this question the method used for the study of the base period will be followed again, that is, one facet of village life will be reviewed at a time, noting the changes that occurred between the time of the original studies and the time of the author's field surveys in 1964. First to be examined are the changes in population.

As table 9 shows, the population of all four villages increased substantially, although not uniformly. Since the experience of the country as a whole was even more striking, the villages' rates of population growth—as shown by the last two columns of the table—failed for the most part to match the nation's rate. The only exception is Soteapan; however, the population of this community shows such marked variations that the accuracy of the data can be questioned. Of the other three villages, the larger increases were registered in Tepoztlán and Mitla. Chan Kom, as will be explained below, might have easily kept pace but for an unusual experience in the late thirties that led to a sizeable out-migration.

5. It will be remembered that in 1930 the population of the country was 16.5 million, that the rural population amounted to 66.6 percent, and that 59.3 percent of the population was illiterate.

TABLE 9

Population of the Villages, Selected Years

VILLAGE	1930	1940	1950	1960	1963	INCREASE FOR PERIOD (%)	AVERAGE ANNUAL INCREASE (%)
Tepoztlán	2,580	3,230	3,900	4,314	5,350	107.3	1.6
Mitla	2,307	2,676	2,882	3,651	4,010	73.8	1.4
Chan Kom	250	270	322	319	386	54.4	1.3
Soteapan	580	1,468	1,965	1,657	....	185.6[a]	3.2[a]
Mexico	16.553[b]	....	....	....	38.416[c]	132.1	2.6

SOURCES: Data from censuses of 1940, 1950, and 1960, and from *U. N. Demographic Yearbook, 1963*; 1963 data for Chan Kom and Mitla from census taken by the local teachers; 1963 data for Tepoztlán from census taken by the municipal authorities.
[a] Figure applies to 1930-60.
[b] Millions.
[c] Estimate (in millions).

It may be wondered if the larger annual growth rate (2.6 percent) shown for Mexico is caused by a larger natural rate of population increase. This is not necessarily so; the difference could be due to net population losses suffered by the villages. This possibly can be made clear with the aid of the additional demographic data presented in table 10.

TABLE 10

Demographic Characteristics of Three Villages, 1963

VILLAGE	BIRTHRATE (per 1,000)	DEATHRATE (per 1,000)	NATURAL POPULATION INCREASE (%)
Tepoztlán	43.70	8.20	3.55
Mitla	50.12	16.04	3.40
Chan Kom	38.80	10.36	2.84
Mexico	45.00	10.40	3.46

SOURCES: Data from the village censuses of 1963 and from *U. N. Demographic Yearbook 1963*. Birthrates and deathrates for the villages computed from the civil register records. These were not available in the case of Soteapan.

The last column of table 10 shows that the natural rates
of population increase for three villages come quite close to
the national rate. In the case of Tepoztlán it is somewhat
higher and for Mitla, slightly lower. The rate for Chan Kom
seems significantly lower, but again this may be a special
case. If these data are compared with the data of table 3, it is
clear that the situation in 1960 was not very different from
the situation in 1930: at that time also the villages' natural
rates of population increase were very close to the nation's natural rate, or higher. It is likely, therefore, that throughout the
1930–63 period there were no significant differences between
the villages' natural rates and the nation's natural rate. This
means that if at the end of the period the relative increase
of the villages' population is below the national increase the
villages must have been net population losers.[6] It is clear
that for both the nation and the villages the natural population rates have gone up considerably.[7] This, as a comparison
with the data of table 3 shows, has not been due to an increase in birthrates, since these have remained more or less
stationary, but to a drastic reduction in deathrates. In
Tepoztlán, for example, the 1930 and 1963 birthrates were
practically the same while the deathrate went down from 22.2
to 8.2 per 1,000. This meant that the rate of natural population increase jumped drastically from 2.1 to 3.55 percent.

In Mitla the demographic changes have not been as pronounced as in Tepoztlán; in the thirties the natural rate of
population increase for the village was already high (2.9
percent), so its advance has not been as marked as in
Tepoztlán. In any case in 1963 the population of Mitla was
increasing via the natural route at a pace almost identical to

6. It is true of course that the comparison rests on crude rates and that
no allowance is made for such factors as infant mortality differentials. However, additional information to be brought out in what follows tends to
support the conclusion that the villages have been net population losers.
7. The increases of the natural population rates (in percentages) have been
the following: Tepoztlán, 69.04; Mitla, 17.24; Mexico, 50.43. The case of
Chan Kom is discussed below.

that of the country. Its birthrate went down (from 56.00 to 50.12 per 1,000) but not enough to match the decrease in the deathrate (from 26.40 to 16.04 per 1,000).

Before examining the case of Chan Kom it may be seen that the natural rates in 1930 were relatively low for both the villages and the country as a whole, but by 1963 they had all been pushed above the 3 percent level. All the birthrates were high in 1930 and they were still high in 1963. The death-rates have gone down, and there are no major differences between the 1963 national deathrate and the deathrates of the villages.

Chan Kom, as indicated above, suffered considerable out-migration and consequently its demographic changes depart somewhat from those of Tepoztlán and Mitla. The out-migra-tion accounts for the low increase in population between 1930 and 1963 (54.4 percent—see table 9). Until the time when this out-migration occurred the population seems to have been increasing rapidly. Redfield, in a second study of Chan Kom in 1948,[8] estimated that the population of the village had reached 445 inhabitants (an increase of 78 per-cent in eighteen years). This growth was interrupted un-expectedly a few years later by internal dissensions traceable to the conversion of some families to Protestantism in the thirties.[9] Until that time everyone had practiced Catholicism, mixed with a certain amount of paganism.

During the years immediately following the conversion there were no serious antagonisms, but as time went on bit-terness and disputes arose that occasionally led to violence. In part the reason was that initially most families embraced Protestantism but gradually some of them returned to Ca-tholicism with the result that the Protestants became a resent-ful minority with reduced opportunities in both an economic

8. Robert Redfield, *A Village That Chose Progress: Chan Kom Revisted* (Chicago: University of Chicago Press, 1950), p. 68.
9. Ibid., p. 88. Redfield gives a detailed account of how the conversion took place.

and a political sense. Resentments and grievances became so strong that in 1938 some Protestant families began to leave Chan Kom. The climax came in 1955 when the old disputes led to an armed confrontation that caused personal injuries. As a result the Protestants left en masse; some establishing themselves in Mérida and others moving to nearby communities with Protestant populations. To Chan Kom this represented a loss of around seventy persons, which explains why the population of the village does not show a marked increase between 1930 and 1963.

The reason for the low birthrate in the village is not clear, but one contributing factor may be a shortage of women. A count taken by the author in May 1964 showed that the village had 409 inhabitants. Of these, 33 were single adult males but there were only 24 potential brides.[10] A consequence of this is that a number of young men need to go outside of Chan Kom to look for wives, and in some cases they fail to return. In addition some young couples have moved to Mérida in search of better opportunities, and while they may be increasing their families, their children have of course been lost to the village.

Chan Kom has also lost young people for a different reason. The village leaders—aware of their own educational inadequacies—have followed the practice of sending their sons to Mérida to be educated. This has been done in the hope that on their return they would become the innovators. Unfortunately what has happened is that once exposed to the lures and comforts of Mérida, they have refused to return.[11]

10. In the elementary school the boys also outnumbered the girls 104 to 82.
11. Mr. Eustaquio Ceme, the outstanding Chan Kom patriarch who has been responsible for so much of the village progress, told the author that this is what happened to one of his sons. After failing on a number of occasions to have this young man return from Mérida, Mr. Ceme had his wife write a letter expressing her apprehension at the possibility of his desiring to marry a city girl if he remained in Mérida. He replied, first, that he had no plans of marrying and, second, that Mérida also had village girls so that should he desire to marry one, it was unnecessary to return to Chan Kom. The parents' pleas failed to bring him back. Other families have had similar experiences.

Turning now to a different aspect of village life, in the following section a review is made of the improvements in communications. Starting with Chan Kom, it can be noted that in 1930 its principal link with the outside world consisted of a twenty-kilometer bush trail that ended at Chichén Itzá. Early in the thirties the villagers became dissatisfied with the trail and consequently decided to build a new one. As a first step they constructed a tower for the purpose of establishing line-of-sight contact with the ruins of Chichén Itzá. This helped the builders make the road as straight as possible.[12] Because of the rough terrain the road was not made perfectly straight, but its length was reduced from twenty to twelve kilometers. It remained in use for some twenty-five years; but then, as a result of some disputes that arose because the road crossed land not belonging to Chan Kom, it had to be abandoned. Once more the villagers set out to build a substitute. This one (still in use) does not end at Chichén Itzá directly but at the paved highway that now joins Mérida with the eastern part of the state of Yucatán. The distance from Chan Kom to the junction with the highway is nine kilometers, and from this junction to Chichén Itzá is four kilometers. In an eastern direction Valladolid is about thirty-five kilometers away.

The present road has been of great importance to Chan Kom; it is a marked improvement over the old bush trail. Accessibility to the village is still difficult, however, because the road passes over many rocky hillocks that make travel by motor vehicle, other than truck, a test of endurance. When it rains, mud makes it even more impassable, and to travel its nine kilometers by truck, even in the absence of serious mishaps, requires about three hours.[13] So once again, aware of the necessity of having an all-weather road suitable

---

12. Redfield, *A Village That Chose Progress,* pp. 16-17.
13. Many people can walk its full length in two and one-half hours. It is so rough that tires do not wear out in the usual manner: after a few trips they become frames of chewed up or shredded rubber.

for all kinds of motor traffic, the villagers started work on its improvement in the spring of 1964. With municipal funds they purchased dynamite to blast some of the hillocks hoping to reduce the road's length to 7.5 kilometers. As on previous occasions the initiative for the work came from the village leaders. The labor was being provided by all the adult males on a communal basis. This time, however, records of expenditures and of hours worked were being kept in the expectation that the state government would pay at least part of the costs. The village leaders had been in contact with their representative in the state legislature, who promised to help them as much as he could. The people of Chan Kom expected that even if state aid was forthcoming they would still have to pay for a share of the cost.[14]

Better communication has also been provided by the post office. This service was inaugurated in 1935 when Chan Kom became the seat of the newly created municipality of the same name. Mail is picked up and delivered at Chichén Itzá three times a week by a young man who makes the trip on bicycle or on foot. For this service he receives a salary of 200 pesos a month. Other communication is provided by the newspapers that arrive for the government officials and teachers. Some of them get a limited circulation. Also, travel to both Mérida and Valladolid has increased considerably and travelers sometimes bring back newspapers. Finally, four families own radios.

In Mitla there have been a number of improvements in communications and transportation. In 1951 the state government built a four-kilometer paved road that joins Mitla with the Pan American Highway. In 1964 another road was under construction in the direction of the mountain villages and it was already being used. Public transportation consisted of

14. The author was told that the cost per paved kilometer was estimated by an engineer at 24,000 pesos. This was not the first time that the villagers had asked for state help to build an all-weather road. Some years ago they made a similar request only to be told that it was impudent to ask for a paved road when at the time not even the city of Valladolid had one.

bus service to Oaxaca and to the eastern part of the country. Freight service was being provided by the trucks and commercial vehicles that arrived at all hours of the day or night. In addition, six persons in the village owned taxis, and they were providing continuous service to Oaxaca and the nearby town of Tlacolula. The mountain road mentioned above had been used by trucks since around 1961, but its traffic increased in 1964 when buses started transporting passengers to the first mountain village twenty-six kilometers away. This road had eliminated the need to keep burros in Mitla since traders were using two different means of transportation: trucks to reach the first mountain village and burros to reach the villages beyond.

It seems that in Mitla the responsibility and the initiative for the construction of the roads have been in the hands of the state government. Mitla has a well-known archeological site which attracts many visitors, both national and foreign.[15] Hence, it is of importance to the state to have a good road between Oaxaca and Mitla. As mentioned above, there is such a road, namely the Pan American Highway and the four-kilometer subsidiary road mentioned above. The paved portion, however, ends on the outskirts of the village. The village itself has no paved streets, and on windy days dust is blown in all directions.

When Parsons did her study there was one bicycle in Mitla, one man owned a truck, and another man owned an automobile. In 1964 it was estimated that bicycles numbered two hundred,[16] and the number of motor vehicles, of all types, had gone up to thirty-two. Radios had become commonplace for poor and rich alike, and in addition two Oaxaca newspapers (with a combined daily circulation of fifty and a

---

15. On a Sunday during a two-hour period, in addition to a bus full of tourists the author counted twenty-three automobiles (some with American license plates) that brought eighty-seven visitors to the ruins.
16. A check at the vehicle registry office in Tlacolula showed that in 1962 Mitla had ninety-two registered bicycles. It is believed that there are as many unregistered.

somewhat larger circulation on Sundays), as well as a number of magazines, were regularly being delivered. Finally, Mitla had its own post office and an airfield which was originally built by the villagers on communal land. After its construction, this airfield was taken over by the federal government, and in 1964 it was used mainly by American missionaries, of whom there was a transient population of from twenty to thirty, including children.

In Soteapan progress in communications had been somewhat slower. It was possible to reach the village by truck, but the use of automobiles was perilous. Three trucks were owned by villagers who used them for the transport of people and merchandise. In 1964 the state government was building a road through the region which was to link many mountain communities with the Veracruz-Mérida highway. Its construction had advanced to within nine kilometers of Soteapan. In spite of the bad roads, wholesale merchants from a town thirty-eight kilometers away were sending their trucks regularly to the village to deliver merchandise. Finally, other improvements in communications include regular postal service and the ownership of radios by many families and by most store owners. Newspapers were read occasionally by a few people.

In Tepoztlán, as in Mitla, there had been many improvements in communications since the base-period survey. The first efforts at road building date from 1929 when some of the village leaders started a campaign to obtain state support for the construction of an eighteen-kilometer road needed to link Tepoztlán with the highway that runs between Mexico City and the state capital (Cuernavaca). As part of these initial efforts some expatriated Tepoztecans residing in Mexico City tried to obtain the assistance of the federal government. This came in 1935 when, during a visit of President Cárdenas to the village, one of the local leaders finally got a definite commitment of federal aid. Shortly after this visit, construction of a paved road started. It was completed and inaugurated the following year and has continued in operation ever since.

This road has played an important role in the life of Tepoztlán; in fact most of the progress that the village has achieved seems to date from its construction. Among other benefits, it has allowed greater commercial interchange and greater mobility of persons. Shortly after it was built, some Tepoztecans organized two cooperatives to provide bus service to the state capital. Both cooperatives were successful and after some time merged. Through the years this group has increased the number of buses and also given employment to a number of people. In 1964 they had extended their service to one more town about thirteen kilometers away. The road that was being used to furnish this service was built in 1963 through the combined efforts of the cooperative and a bus transportation company that provides direct first-class service from Mexico City to Tepoztlán and the region beyond. In 1964 the federal government was building a superhighway that was going to pass through Tepoztlán. It was intended to serve as a link between two major highways, but Tepoztlán stood to gain even greater accessibility.

Another new means of communication found in the village in 1964 was the telephone.[17] It was first installed by the federal government in 1956 and originally there were only six subscribers. By 1964, however, the number had increased to twenty-three. Newspapers were being bought by a few people in the state capital, and occasionally enterprising newsboys were coming to the village to sell them, especially when they carried news of local interest. The number of radios in 1943 was not more than four;[18] by 1956 there were eighty of them (battery-operated since there was no electricity), and in 1964 (with electricity already introduced) only very poor people did not own one. Television had also made

---

17. Oscar Lewis, *Tepoztlán: Village in Mexico* (New York: Henry Holt & Co., 1960), p. 100.
18. Ibid.

its appearance. Tepoztlán was getting reception from one or two Mexico City channels, and a few families and commercial establishments had already purchased TV sets.

The progress of the villages in education is examined next. Table 11 gives some data about the 1964 educational situa-

TABLE 11

Educational Characteristics of the Villages, 1964

VILLAGE	NUMBER OF SCHOOLS	NUMBER OF TEACHERS	NUMBER OF PUPILS
Tepoztlán	8	53[a]	1,989
Mitla	1	14	653
Chan Kom	1	2	80
Soteapan	1	3	. . . .

[a] Approximate figure.

tion of the communities. Improvement in educational facilities has varied from village to village, but it has occurred in all of them. In their efforts the villagers have had the assistance of some programs of the federal government, such as the distribution of free textbooks among the elementary schools. In Mitla, Chan Kom, and Soteapan the native languages were still widely used in 1964, but it was difficult to find persons who did not speak or understand Spanish. In Tepoztlán, Nahuatl had become rare. If the data of table 11 are compared with the data of table 4, it can readily be seen that in Tepoztlán the number of both schools and teachers had risen sharply since 1930. In Mitla the number of teachers had also gone up, although the village still had only one school. Chan Kom had in 1930 a very modest school and only one teacher. In 1931, using communal labor and their own resources, the villagers began work on a new masonry two-room school.[19] During construction this building collapsed, killing one man and injuring several others, but the project was not abandoned. A second start was made and a school was finally built.

19. Redfield, *A Village That Chose Progress,* pp. 17-18.

It remained in operation until 1962, when the present one was begun. For the construction of this latest school, the villagers were able to enlist the support of the state and federal governments. Chan Kom itself contributed the land and about 9,000 pesos. Of this sum, 1,300 pesos came from a per capita tax of 10 pesos levied on 130 adult males, 2,000 pesos came as a contribution from the ejido authorities, and the rest came from the municipal treasury. The state government donated tiles, and the federal government donated the prefabricated structure, a small electric generator, and a movie projector. In 1964 the first five elementary grades were being taught by two teachers.

Redfield reports that in 1944 a cultural mission sent by the federal government visited Chan Kom.[20] It consisted of ten people who remained in the village for a period of about sixteen months teaching carpentry, bread baking, leatherworking, music, hygiene, and the digging of water wells. They also carried out some agricultural programs and built another outdoor theater—one had already been built at the initiative of a teacher. Through the years the knowledge of Spanish has increased and the number of illiterates has gone down. Out of the 386 persons counted by the teachers in 1963, only 49 adults (mostly women) indicated inability to read. The interest of the villagers in culture, moreover, is of long standing. Since they first came in contact with the American archeologists at Chichén Itzá in the late twenties, it has been their practice to seek new visitors. This has been a rewarding endeavor; through the years they have been hosts to many distinguished scholars who have come to the village to lecture on various practical subjects. The modern school, therefore, represented in 1964 the culmination of an old and continuous interest in culture.

Soteapan has had the uninterrupted service of a teacher since 1948. When this teacher first arrived the local leaders

20. Ibid., pp. 20-21, 48.

made plans for the construction of a new school. Their efforts,
however, ran into the opposition of many parents who feared
that the school would make their children lazy. Not until
1955 were the plans carried out and the school built. For its
construction, in addition to the labor of many men who
worked without pay, Soteapan also contributed 13,500 pesos
from its municipal treasury and from various assessments on
individuals. The state government donated construction
materials, and up until 1964 it had also been paying the
salaries of the three teachers who worked in the school. Students wishing to go on to high school had to go to the nearest
city, which is Minatitlán. Finally, in 1964 there was at least
one student (the son of the most prosperous merchant)
attending college in Mexico City.

Mitla, as was indicated above, still had only one school.
This was built through the cooperation of the townspeople
in the late thirties and was enlarged in 1955–56, at which
time four classrooms were added. Since that time the number
of both teachers and pupils has risen sharply.

Some years ago many parents in Mitla tended to take their
children out of school after they finished the third grade. To
correct this condition a committee had been in operation to
make sure that children in the higher grades remained in
school. Those parents who put their children to work before
they finished the sixth grade were being put in jail one or
two days, to make them "reconsider." The school facilities
had become inadequate to take care of all the children of
school age—919 of them were counted in the census taken by
the teachers in 1963; nevertheless, during a period of a few
days after the opening of the 1964 school year, the principal
used the village's public address system to exhort parents
to send their children to school. There were thirteen groups
in grades from one to six; in the first grade there were five
groups and an equal number of boys and girls, but in the
higher grades the number of groups became smaller and the
boys tended to outnumber the girls. The school was being

supported by the federal government, although Mitla was contributing 150 pesos a month toward the payment of one of the teachers and it was also contributing the crop of an eight-hectare alfalfa plot which was communally cultivated.

In 1964 plans had already been made for the construction of a new school. This one was to include, among other things, a dining room where breakfasts would be served. The land had been acquired, and pledges of state and federal aid had been obtained. Mitla's contribution to the project was estimated to run into several thousand pesos. During a visit to the village the wife of the Mexican president had offered to pay for the construction costs, but until the spring of 1964 no final arrangements had been made and actual construction had not started. As a final note it may be added that in 1963 there were thirty-three students in the graduating class. Of these, eleven had gone to high school in Oaxaca and three more were commuting daily to Tlacolula's high school, twelve kilometers away. It seems that all the teachers, with one exception, made their homes in Oaxaca and traveled daily to work.

Moving on to the case of Tepoztlán, table 11 shows that its educational progress has been outstanding. Lewis reported that in 1956 the village already had four elementary schools with an enrollment of over 900, and one high school with an enrollment of 110.[21] In 1964 the enrollment of the latter had reached 352, the number of elementary schools had gone up to six, and their combined enrollment had gone up to 1,410. In addition, a new kindergarten was in operation with a staff of ten teachers who took care of 227 children.[22] Out of the total enrollment of 1,989 in the village schools, there were 1,038 boys and 951 girls. Most of the students were residents of Tepoztlán, but some came from other villages, especially

21. O. Lewis, *Tepoztlán,* p. 99.
22. This kindergarten was inaugurated in 1960. Before this time two teachers working under makeshift arrangements took care of a few pre-school-age children.

to the high school, which had a few boys and girls from various mountain communities.[23]

In their educational efforts the people of Tepoztlán had been able to enlist the help of influential friends.[24] They also had had the cooperation of the state and the federal governments. This outside assistance together with their own work and initiative had been the main factors behind their advances in education. The largest elementary school, for example, came into being through this sort of cooperation. It is reported that the Mexican president once met with World War II veterans from all parts of the country. He asked whether there was anything that the government could do for them, and a boy from Tepoztlán suggested, and got, the school.[25]

Through the years attendance in this school has increased and federal support has continued. In 1964 breakfasts were being served to the poorest children.[26] In addition, plans had been made to set up shops for the teaching of trades. Most children who finished elementary school were continuing on to high school, but those unable to go on were expected to benefit from this program. The principal was aware of

23. Some of these high school students had to travel almost three hours each way in order to attend school. The YMCA, with the aid of a Sears and Roebuck grant, was operating part of its Tepoztlán camp as a residence for eleven of these students. In this camp the students—at an annual cost of 1,500 pesos per student—were provided with all their requirements. Additional quarters were under construction, and it was expected that assistance would be available to a total of twenty-five students. Others, unfortunately, had to continue their daily trek.

24. Tepoztlán has attracted visitors for many years, since in addition to its natural beauty it has an archeological site and an ancient church and convent (now a national museum). Since the opening of the road the number of visitors has increased and from them Tepoztlán has drawn most of its important friends—both Mexican and foreign. Some of these friends have simply been visitors, others have built homes there.

25. This man, now a teacher, saw action in the South Pacific in World War II. He was a member of the air squadron that Mexico sent there as part of its contribution to the war.

26. Some of the breakfasts were being paid by private sponsors who had established homes in the village; outstanding among them were a Mexican banker and an American industrialist.

the fact that some industry had been coming to the state capital and that in some cases workers had to be completely trained by the new employers. Consequently, he thought that it would be easier for the youth of Tepoztlán to find jobs in industry if when they left school they already had some mechanical training.

The opening of the high school also required initiative and work on the part of the people of Tepoztlán. For this project, the first steps were taken by three men who solicited help from the federal government and from the well-known Mexican poet Carlos Pellicer. After this beginning a committee was formed to take over many of the negotiations, which eventually met with success as both federal and state aid were procured. A former elementary school which was no longer in use was made ready and classes began in 1950. A year later new steps were taken to get a better building and again the expectations were realized. A new school was built with federal aid on land that had previously belonged to the Catholic church. During its first years of operation, since government aid was not enough to cover expenses, parents were required to pay a registration fee of sixty pesos and tuition of twenty-five pesos a month. In 1962 the federal government took full charge of the school and, among other actions, practically eliminated the financial burden of the parents. In addition to the usual courses, the school was providing vocational training. It had eight sewing machines, a lathe, and various types of tools, and steps were being taken by parents and teachers to procure more equipment. Ten of the students had received scholarships provided by a private sponsor.[27]

27. The sponsor was the same American mentioned in the previous footnote. Besides sponsoring scholarships and paying for school breakfasts, this man has done many other things for Tepoztlán. Included among them are the following: donation of a sports field, donation of a piano to one of the schools, and a contribution toward the purchase of water carriers to supply the public fountains. He had also helped a nearby village get electricity. In 1964 he agreed to pay for the graduation expenditures of twelve local boys and girls who were to receive college degrees.

For some educational projects Tepoztlán was fortunate in being able to rally the support of a high government official in Mexico's Ministry of Education. This man was instrumental in getting aid for several schools. For the new kindergarten, for instance, he was able to obtain federal funds to construct and furnish the building, the land having been provided by the village. He was also instrumental in getting the federal government to pay for the teachers' salaries. The only charges that were being levied on the parents were a matriculation fee of five pesos and tuition of three pesos a month, both of which were needed to pay for the materials used by the children.

As far as higher education is concerned, there has always been a number of high school graduates who leave Tepoztlán to continue their schooling. Some move to Mexico City and some move to the state capital. There is a drawback to this because they do not come back to the village once they complete their studies. Some find that Tepoztlán offers no opportunity for the practice of their professions, others become attached to urban living and settle in the city, and others are sent to other parts of the country by their urban employers.[28] In spite of this the village does not suffer from a complete lack of talent, because professionals from other parts of the country (such as doctors, teachers, veterinarians, agronomists, etc.) come to Tepoztlán to render their services. In 1964 many of the teachers and the two resident doctors, for example, were not native Tepoztecans. On balance, however, Tepoztlán seemed to be a net exporter of educated people.

When some villagers were asked by the author why they were so concerned with progress in education when they knew that those whom they helped tended to move away, the reply was that from among those helped, one would some-

28. O. Lewis, *Tepoztlán*, p. 97, noted that in 1956 Tepoztlán was already exporting talent. There were more Tepoztecan teachers than it was possible to employ, and consequently seventy of them were working in other communities. In 1964 Tepoztlán was still exporting teachers.

day emerge who would take an interest in the affairs of the village. This hope was realized in 1964 when a young Tepoztecan, a mechanical engineer who was working at a sugar mill, was prevailed upon to run for the presidency and won. So Tepoztlán had for the first time a professional native son as president. The village also seemed to derive some benefit from those who left because most of them made remittances to their families. Then, there were a few who did try to do something for Tepoztlán. In 1963, for instance, a cultural association of young expatriates opened the first library with books collected from various sources.

For reasons that will be more fully explored in the following chapter, it seems unavoidable that Tepoztlán should suffer a loss of professional people, especially in view of the lack of opportunities for the practice of some professions. But there is another loss that is almost as serious—the young people who finish either elementary or high school and find no employment in Tepoztlán. In some cases the land still offers opportunity to a few. A prosperous farmer, for example, may be able to utilize the services of his son. Then there are some who become tradesmen and are thus able to make a living in the village; but others, including some young men with vocational training, find no work and hence have to turn to the city for employment.

It will be remembered that in the thirties none of the villages had a doctor and that they lacked other health facilities. In the last few years the situation has changed, and all of them (with the exception of Chan Kom) have witnessed the introduction of various medical services. Mitla has had a resident doctor since 1950. Partly as the result of his work there had been a noticeable reduction in the mortality rate. In addition the federal government had been establishing centers of rural hygiene throughout the country, and one of them was opened in Mitla in 1961. There was a registered nurse in charge of it and once a week a doctor came from

Oaxaca. The services that were being provided by the center included first aid, preventive medicine, vaccinations, prenatal and postnatal care, nutrition instruction, distribution of food (including wheat, powdered milk, butter, etc.) to poor children of less than six years of age, instruction to young girls on home economics, and instruction to mothers on ways to improve their homes. These services were being provided gratis, although in some cases minimal sums were charged. It was expected in 1964 that a new center, complete with sanitarium, would soon be opened. To conclude the changes in health care it may be added that since 1963 Mitla has had a drugstore.

In Soteapan a center of rural hygiene similar to the one in Mitla was opened in 1964. This one was housed in a prefabricated structure which was erected near the center of the village. It had a resident doctor and a nurse and offered services similar to those provided in Mitla. When emergencies arose, or when patients required special care, ambulances came from the city of Minatitlán, which is about thirty-five kilometers away.

Tepoztlán has had a resident doctor and a druggist for a number of years.[29] In 1964 it had two doctors and a health center similar to those mentioned above. This health center was inaugurated in 1962, and its staff consisted of one of the local doctors assisted by three full-time nurses. Many persons were taking advantage of it, but since there is considerable ease of communication with the state capital, some Tepoztecans were going there for medical care.

Municipal services constitute another area in which there has been noticeable progress in the villages. In the case of Chan Kom, the following improvements can be listed. In 1963 electricity was introduced. The service at the time of the author's visit was being provided free of charge and only on special occasions. The equipment consisted of a small

29. Ibid., p. 96.

generator donated by the federal government. In 1964 only the houses and the streets in the center of the village had been connected to the distribution network. To pay for the installation the adult males were taxed 10 pesos per person, the ejido authorities contributed 2,000 pesos, and the municipal treasury contributed 3,000 pesos. The quality of the installation left much to be desired, but the people of Chan Kom were occasionally enjoying the benefits of electricity.

There had been no modernization in the water supply, although the number of private wells had gone up. Redfield noted in 1948 that there were fourteen wells, twelve of which had been dug since 1931.[30] By 1964 the number had increased to thirty-one.

One of the early ambitions of the leaders of Chan Kom was to make their village the seat of a new municipality, and in the pursuit of this goal they spent considerable effort. For example, they presented a series of petitions to the state government, as a result of which a post office and a civil registry office were opened in 1935. The public building used for the municipal offices and two churches, one Catholic and one Protestant, also date from this time. The former church had continued in service, but the latter, although still in good repair, had been unused since the departure of the Protestants. Chan Kom still had one of its old outdoor theaters, and part of its ample main square was used as a baseball field.

In Soteapan in 1961 a new municipal building, costing 72,000 pesos, was constructed. To pay for it municipal funds were used that had been accumulated for this purpose for a number of years. These funds were supplemented by contributions from the people, who also provided the labor on a communal basis. In the last few years a bandstand and a pavillion were also built, partly by communal labor and partly with the monetary contributions of the villagers. When a public project is being considered, a committee is

30. Redfield, *A Village That Chose Progress*, p. 33.

usually appointed to see that it is carried out. One of the first activities of the committee is to conduct a public meeting in which it is decided how much each inhabitant must contribute. The assessment of a poor farmer may be as low as 25 pesos, whereas a prosperous merchant may be assessed 200 pesos or more. Those in charge of the assessments are usually persons who know the condition of each family and are therefore expected to fix the assessments in an equitable manner. In 1964 the church was being rebuilt and already several thousand pesos had been spent. In this instance besides the local contributions others had been obtained from nearby communities. Finally, the electrical distribution system had been improved and extended. Old cables and fixtures had been replaced, and power lines had been run to parts of the village that had previously been without electricity. In 1941 only one man had electric service in his home, but by 1953 sixteen percent of the population had electricity and this number had increased since then.

In Tepoztlán the water system has been the object of considerable attention. In the late forties a plan was put into effect to supply water to private homes and to a number of public taps. To finance this project each house was assessed twenty pesos.[31] Those who became users and had the service installed were charged an additional ten pesos a month, and those who used the public taps were charged four pesos a month. By the early fifties this project had become so costly that the villagers had to ask for federal aid. This was granted but in the process the government assumed control of the system. In 1964 with more people and a larger number of houses (some of which, especially those built by outsiders, had swimming pools), water had become scarce. The spring that had traditionally supplied the water became inadequate, and to remedy the situation the federal government was in the process of digging a large well and also installing pipes of larger diameter.

31. There were about one thousand houses at that time.

Public improvements in Tepoztlán, and to some extent in Mitla, have usually been village-wide. At times, however, works have been undertaken at the neighborhood level. In 1949, for instance, before Tepoztlán went to work on its main water system, one of its neighborhoods installed a small water network, which included a few taps for public use. The neighborhood residents donated the labor, and some help came from the governments of Mexico and the United States, as well as from the Dirección de Cooperación Interamericana de Salubridad Pública. Sometimes improvements have also been made in the neighborhood chapels, usually under the direction of the mayordomos in charge of them. For these improvements the neighborhood residents make contributions of money, labor, or both. In 1964 the street in front of one of these chapels was surfaced with concrete, and prior to this two other neighborhood chapels had been redecorated. Around one of the latter a fence had also been erected. Finally, the elementary schools that have been opened in different neighborhoods owe their existence in large measure to the work and initiative of the neighborhood parents.

The introduction of electricity has been another important improvement in Tepoztlán. During the early fifties various attempts were made to obtain federal and state aid for this purpose, but they were unsuccessful. To complicate matters there were many people, both inside and outside Tepoztlán, who opposed electrification fearing that the village would lose its rustic charm. In 1957, the then municipal secretary, assisted by two employees of the federal power commission in Mexico City, approached the electric company with a request for service. Cost estimates were made and it was found that the work required expenditures in excess of half a million pesos. It was agreed that the municipal authorities would ask for a contribution of 100 pesos from every house owner and that this money would be turned over to the company as the village's share of the cost. A committee

was formed to coordinate the work and soon thereafter it
started collecting the money.[32] When 45,000 pesos had been
collected and paid to the company, it took over the collec-
tions directly, thus assuming full responsibility for the work.
The service was inaugurated in 1958. Since that time the
company—with headquarters in Mexico City—has been
nationalized, and it is not clear whether all the house owners
ever paid the 100 pesos in full. Until 1964 no public lighting
had been installed; the only public lighting available consisted of a few light bulbs that some house owners had installed outside their homes. The reason given for this condition was lack of municipal funds. In those parts of the village
that had no service, if the people were willing to pay for the
post, cables were run to it and connections were then made
to the houses.

In spite of the fact that at times its activities have been
viewed with suspicion by some people, in the last few years
the YMCA has played a large role in the affairs of Tepoztlán.
Its first activity dates from the early forties when it opened
a boys' camp and embarked on a program of rural development. To put the program into effect, the local organization
enlisted the support of the International YMCA and, to take
charge of the program, obtained the services of Dr. Spencer
Hatch, who had done rural reconstruction work in India.[33]

The program included the following activities: restoration
of the fertility of the soil (which after being analyzed began
to be treated with compost made from weeds and waste
material), experimentation with seventy new crops and
twenty-one varieties of trees, experimentation with livestock
and poultry (including pigs, goats, bulls, sheep, chickens,
and ducks),[34] experimentation with bees, instruction to

32. Some house-owners paid their assessments in one lump sum, but the
majority made payment in installments.
33. Spencer Hatch, "Rural Reconstruction in Mexico," *Agriculture in the
Americas* 4, no. 3 (March 1944), p. 51, gives an account of the purpose and
operation of the program.
34. Some of these experiments were carried out with the cooperation of the
Rockefeller Foundation.

women on knitting and weaving, instruction and building of model homes,[35] and organization of various social activities. As time went on other programs were added, such as the formation of children's clubs; instruction on homemaking, sanitation, and hygiene;[36] an enlarged athletic schedule; a day nursery; the teaching of crop rotation; and the housing and support of students from neighboring communities.

It is difficult to establish how much was accomplished by these programs because Tepoztlán was subjected to many influences other than those that the work of the YMCA may have exerted. Some activities did not seem successful at the time. This was the case, for instance, of the knitting and weaving instruction program. At one time it seemed on the road to success because many women had enrolled and were making sweaters, quilts, and other goods. These products were usually sold by the YMCA in Mexico City, and part of the proceeds were turned over to the trainees. A labor leader discovered what was taking place and tried to unionize the women. As a result of this the program was discontinued and the shop was dismantled. The looms—about twelve of them —were given to the trainees, most of whom sold them later on. So far as it is known only one woman kept hers, which she was still using in 1964.

The people were also taught how to make latrines, but as in the previous case, this did not seem to have much effect at the time. Other failures were the abandonment of some crops that were attacked by pests and the abandonment of the beehives that were damaged by a black fly—which, incidentally, also damaged some of the experimental trees. The poultry and livestock improvement programs did not

35. A model home of whitewashed adobe was actually built in the camp. It had windows, a stovepipe, a shower, and rustic beds. It also had an attached barn and a small plot with fruit trees. Its cost was modest, and it was built in the hope that after the villagers saw it they would build similar homes—which a few of them did.

36. At one time, as part of this program, brigades were brought to Tepoztlán to treat the sick, administer vaccinations, and give instruction on natal care, hygiene, and sanitation.

seem to have the desired effects either.[37] Yet, in spite of the YMCA's seeming failures, in Tepoztlán today new crops are being grown, crop rotation is practiced, fertilizer is used, some families raise large quantities of good quality poultry, some farmers own good quality livestock, and many improvements have been introduced in housebuilding. How much of all this is due to the work of the YMCA is difficult to say because, as mentioned above, other factors have also played a role. What is certain is that the efforts of the YMCA have been costly. A YMCA publication gives a rough idea of the cost of the various programs, including the operation of the boys' camp.[38] It shows that for 1956 the budgeted expenditures amounted to 172,809 pesos. The anticipated income—from operation of the camp, use of the swimming pool, sale of various products, dues, etc—was 110,600 pesos. This left an apparent deficit of 62,209 pesos to be made up from other sources. Of course it should be kept in mind that the YMCA did not direct its work toward economic improvement exclusively, but in any case its development programs seem to have required large sums of money.

Hatch observed some resistance to the introduction of innovations, although when a project produced the sought after results and these offered the possibility of profitable application, the villagers tended to show great interest. Their stubborness, however, could at times be carried to extremes. Hatch wrote: "Stubborness is a virtue with them. They cannot be induced to do something they do not want to do or do not believe in. Offer them money many times the value of a piece of land, a donkey, or a duck, and it tempts them not at all if they have decided not to sell."[39]

37. In order to improve the quality of the poultry, at the outset of the project fine quality chicks were given to the people free of charge. This did not seem to arouse noticeable interest and consequently an exchange program was instituted which consisted of a one-for-one exchange of ordinary chickens or eggs for their respective good quality equivalents.
38. "III Conferencia Nacional Consultativa de Asociaciones Christianas de Jóvenes de la República Mexicana," mimeographed (Torreón, 1955), pp. 12-14.
39. Hatch, "Rural Reconstruction," p. 53. The author had the opportunity

Both American and Mexican companies have come to Tepoztlán to make a number of movies, and on some occasions they have made contributions toward the improvement of the public facilities. A Mexican producer, for instance, paid for the paving of the main square. Unfortunately, in the last few years the governors of the state have directed these funds in their own direction. In 1964 they were giving permits for the use of the village so that when the producers arrived they felt under no obligation to make a local contribution.

The improvement of the municipal services in Mitla has followed a pattern similar to that of Tepoztlán. Some projects have required no outside assistance, but for the more costly ones help from both the state and the federal governments has been necessary. When a project is being considered, the authorities usually conduct a public meeting at which a commitment to cooperate is obtained from the people. Then a committee is named and put in charge while another committee takes on the job of deciding how much each working adult and each business must contribute. When outside assistance is sought, prolonged and unusual maneuvers may be resorted to by those in charge of a project. For the construction of the water system, for example, the negotiations were carried on by two men. First they wrote letters to various governmental agencies in Mexico City until they found the one handling requests for aid such as theirs. Then they began corresponding with this agency and in addition started sending boxes of cheese and pork to the man in charge. To insure that the gifts reached the intended recipient, they also made similar shipments to the official's home. In all, these two men

---

to test the nonpecuniary strain of the people during his visit to Tepoztlán. A man purchased a horse some years ago for 1,500 pesos. It turned out to be a fast horse, and at various festivals the owner won many races. Although the horse did not race anymore, some of the man's friends had offered to buy it. When the man was asked why he did not sell the horse while it was still possible to get some money for it, he replied, "What? After a good service a bad reward?" thus indicating his displeasure at any suggestion of his parting with a horse that had given him much enjoyment.

spent more than 3,000 pesos out of their own pockets before federal aid was finally obtained.[40] The state government also cooperated, and the water system was finally installed and inaugurated in 1959.[41] At the time of the author's visit service was being provided to thirty-eight private homes and to one public fountain.

Prior to the inauguration of this system the people used a network of pipes that was installed in the thirties between the "white water" springs and five public fountains. This network was still in operation in 1964 since most families had not yet taken advantage of the new service—some because they had wells in their homes, others because they could get water from the public fountains, and others because they thought that the monthly charge of twenty pesos was too high. In spite of the modernization of the system, water scarcity had continued, and during some months the service was available only for particular hours of the morning and evening.

Another public improvement was the introduction of electricity in 1961. It will be remembered that one of Mitla's wealthy men had furnished electricity since the time of Parson's study (see chapter 2). This service, which was given for only a few hours in the evening, had been discontinued around 1957. As in the case of the new water system, Mitla received aid from both the state and federal governments.[42] In 1964 there were 377 private consumers and in addition there was a public lighting system. The annual operating cost

40. It may be wondered whether graft of this type is normally required to get government aid. Although graft in government circles is not unknown, of all the government aid requests reported to the author, this was the only one that involved this type of action. It may be added that the "gifts" were voluntary and that the two men, wise perhaps to the ways of the world, took the initiative.
41. The contribution of the federal government amounted to 236,000 pesos; that of the state government to 36,000 pesos; and that of private contributors (mainly the local people) to 25,300 pesos.
42. According to the municipal authorities, Mitla contributed 100,000 pesos, and the federal government 247,100 pesos. The contribution of the state government was 115,500 pesos.

of the latter amounted to 10,800 pesos; a sum which was being paid from special assessments on commercial establishments and from a municipal allowance of 1,200 pesos per year.

Other public improvements may be added to the list, among them: the construction of a concrete bridge in 1959 (for this project Mitla had the help of the state government), the construction of the present marketplace in 1934–35, the rebuilding of another bridge in 1949, the building of a bandstand and tower with a clock (the old one, constructed in 1941–42, was destroyed by an earthquake), and improvements in the main square, toward which the merchants donated some benches. Since 1950 Mitla has had a museum of Zapotecan art which was founded by an American couple. In 1959 it was sold to Mexico City College, which continued its operation. The museum had an adjoining hotel and restaurant, catering mainly to tourists. Its register showed thirty-two visitors on a Sunday and an average of fifteen visitors per day—on the basis of one week's observations. Lastly, the church had also undergone a number of repairs and improvements.

It was mentioned in chapter 2 that in the thirties there were in the villages some men who made a living by the practice of specialized occupations but that agriculture was by far the most important economic activity. The dominance of agriculture had continued, but through the years other activities had undergone expansion. In Soteapan in 1941, for example, people showed little interest in trade; but in 1964 there were nine "large" stores (plus numerous smaller ones), and their operation had become a full-time occupation. Too, since 1962 the village had had a corn-grinding mill (not used by many women who still preferred to grind their corn by hand), and since 1961 it had had a small factory that made ice cream popsicles. At the same time people had shown growing interest in transportation as a business, and at various times trucks had been purchased for business purposes.

Chan Kom had its first corn mill in 1941.[43] By 1946 it had two of them and the number of stores had gone up to four. Between 1946 and 1964, however, the number of these establishments remained the same, probably due to the population loss caused by the religious conflict. One activity had had a great impact on the life of the village—the breeding of cattle and hogs. The speed with which this activity grew in importance can be gathered from the fact that in 1931 Chan Kom had "perhaps two score head of cattle";[44] by 1948, however, the number had increased to between four and five hundred and the number of hogs had registered a rise of similar magnitude. In 1931, moreover, cattle were acquired for their prestige value, but in 1948 cattle had become an important business. Along with the cattle trade, considerable activity also developed in corn and hogs with the end result that Chan Kom became the center of the hog, corn, and cattle trade in the region.

Redfield believed that the main factors behind the upsurge of trade were: the improvement of trails, the ability of the villagers to learn and imitate the operations of visiting merchants, and the advantage that the people of Chan Kom had over the people of neighboring communities in possessing larger amounts of savings which could be put to work in trade.

In 1964 the breeding of cattle and hogs had continued to receive attention and the ownership of both was widespread.[45] Setbacks had also occurred from time to time, the most recent one being an epizootic of hogs in 1963–64 which

43. Redfield, *A Village That Chose Progress*, pp. 20-21.
44. Ibid., pp. 51-54.
45. Mr. Ceme and five of his sons alone owned ninety-nine head of cattle. The author was told that when Redfield and his family were in Chan Kom in 1948 they employed a native woman as maid. With the money she received as wages she bought a calf. Her investment paid off because by 1964 it had turned into twelve head of cattle.

killed some 400 of them. Thus while Chan Kom—and for that matter the other villages as well—managed to make advances in trade, cattle breeding, and other fields, the advancement always happened in the face of the hostile environment and other opposing factors. As will be made clear in the final chapter, various growth-retarding elements have been at work slowing down the progress of the villages—a fact that makes their achievements the more remarkable.

As an occupation, the practice of beekeeping had changed somewhat. In 1964 only one person kept a few beehives. The reason was that an outsider was given a twenty-year monopolistic concession to keep beehives within Chan Kom's boundaries. On each of the approximately one thousand beehives that he had installed, he had to pay to the ejido authorities a tax of one peso a year; he also had to pay fifteen pesos to the municipal authorities on each container of honey that he took out of the village boundaries. The number of the latter varied between 100 and 120 containers per year. The funds that were thus being collected by the community were earmarked for a public improvement fund.

Other nonagricultural activities among Chan Kom villagers include the construction of ovens by three men who baked bread occasionally and the purchase of two trucks by another man, who became so successful that he later moved out of the village and had his trucks operating on the transisthmian highway that connects the Gulf of Mexico with the Pacific Ocean. Two other villagers had also purchased trucks and were providing service to Mérida two or three times a week. Both of them were residing in Mérida, although they still participated actively in the affairs of Chan Kom.[46]

Activity in housing had continued. In 1931 there were nine masonry houses and four more were under construction, but by 1964 the number had gone up to thirty-three.

46. In addition to those persons actually engaged in transportation, two of the most prosperous merchants indicated to the author their intention to buy trucks upon completion of the improvements to the road.

In spite of this increase there were no full-time masons; since houses were built by families with the help of relatives and friends, there was no need for them. A few families were still making hammocks, rope, and baskets, although the latter were made only occasionally and mainly for the family's own use. Other families had forgotten these crafts. Years ago there were some people who made straw hats, but in 1964 hats could be purchased for three pesos and nobody found it profitable to stay away from his cornfield for one day in order to make a hat. Hence, hats were no longer being made in Chan Kom. Finally, a few years ago there were two musical groups, but with the departure of the Protestants the number was reduced to one.

It was indicated in chapter 2 that in Mitla commercial activities have always been important. With the increase in population and with better communications, commerce has acquired an even greater importance. In 1964 the number of stores (of all sizes) had increased to sixty. There were six corn mills, two small distilleries, seven weaving shops (where skirts, shawls, belts, blouses, etc., were being made on hand looms),[47] six wholesale grain merchants, three restaurants, two hotels, a popsicle factory, a tailor shop, several barbershops, and a gasoline service station. Most farmers were still making trading trips after the agricultural season, and many families (with or without the aid of hired help) were still making woolen shawls, clay figures, and hand-embroidered pieces of clothing which they sold to tourists or in Oaxaca. Six men owned taxis, and twenty-two others owned trucks or other commercial vehicles of various types.

A few years ago many men had the opportunity to go to work in the United States as temporary farm laborers. Many of them, in fact, made several trips. If a man was careful with

---

47. The largest shop employed six men. All the shops depended on the purchases of the tourists who came to the village; however the largest shop was seeking orders not only in Oaxaca and Mexico City but also in the cities of the northern part of the country.

his expenditures, he was able to save around one hundred dollars a month, that is, a sum which could reach around five thousand pesos a season. Part of this money was regularly sent home for the support of the families, but part was saved and thus on their return many of these men were able to build new homes or purchase livestock, pack animals, radios, bicycles, wristwatches, clothes, sewing machines, etc. Since in 1964 the United States was in the process of stopping the importation of farm labor from Mexico, this source of employment had practically disappeared. To conclude, there is no doubt that the number of nonagricultural occupations and the number of persons employed outside agriculture had increased. The cottage industries seemed to be the same as those mentioned in chapter 2, but two of them (weaving and liquor distilling) had acquired commercial importance.

Tepoztlán had undergone changes in its nonagricultural activities somewhat similar to those of Mitla. The number of commercial establishments of all types (stores, dry cleaners, tailors, flower merchants, corn mills, etc.) had increased to more than thirty-five. The village had one resort hotel and a second under construction, two saloons with billiard tables, a few places that sold liquor, a cinema (operated by a man who worked in the United States as a farm laborer), a boy-scout camp, and many new houses, both of outsiders and of Tepoztecans.

Increased activity in housing meant that masons, painters, and carpenters had more work. Also, more women were in the labor force—as teachers, clerical employees, dressmakers, beauticians, etc. Lewis noted that already in 1956 the number of nonagricultural occupations had increased to thirty-three and that the number of people employed in them had reached 565.[48] If these figures are compared with the corresponding ones of table 7 (sixteen nonagricultural occupations, sixty-six people employed in them in 1926–27), it can be seen that

48. O. Lewis, *Tepoztlán,* p. 97.

there was a marked expansion in nonagricultural activities. Moreover, it seems that this expansion had continued from 1956 to the time of the author's survey.

Many of the outsiders who had built homes in Tepoztlán came only on weekends or holidays. Usually they brought their own food, isolated themselves in their homes, and took no active part in the village economy. To the extent that they paid taxes, Tepoztlán derived some benefit from their presence, although the real estate tax (which is the most important) is a state and not a local tax. A further benefit provided by them was the employment which they gave to servants, gardeners, or caretakers. Too, a few of them had become interested in the local affairs and made contributions toward the improvement of the village. Apart from this, the influx of these weekend residents had two noticeable effects: a marked increase of land prices and a reduction of arable land. These effects, moreover, were already apparent in the fifties. Lewis noticed that whereas in 1943 only a few people were willing to sell their land, in the middle fifties a relatively large number of land sales took place.[49] In 1964 the trend had continued, and in this year many Tepoztecans sold land to an outside corporation that intended to use it for a golf course. Thus, while some people had sold their land, others had found themselves without plots on which to build their houses or plant their crops. This situation became so acute that it prompted the federal government and the ejido authorities to distribute plots on the slopes of the mountains to needy people, who after paying only a minimal sum could then build homes there.

The improvement in transportation, and the consequent ease of travel, had allowed many workers (both men and women) to find jobs outside the village. Some men had found seasonal employment in the sugar mills of the state, while others had found work as laborers in Cuernavaca and Mexico City. A number of persons were making a living in

49. Ibid., pp. 98-99.

transportation (both passenger and freight), and some men had found work in road construction. The company that was building the superhighway through Tepoztlán employed about fifty men from the village. It could have employed more, but it had a number of workers from other parts of the country whom it kept on a more or less permanent basis. Furthermore, many road building operations were mechanized so that bulldozers and earth-moving equipment had further reduced the need for local labor.

The movie companies that came to the village were a source of temporary employment. A man who worked as an extra earned twenty pesos a day, and a somewhat larger sum if he used his horse. A few occupations were on the decline, among them charcoal making. In the thirties this occupation provided employment to a number of men who worked in the mountain forests with a minimum of equipment, their most expensive item being the burros that transported the charcoal. In the forties and fifties the forests that supplied their raw materials came to be closely watched by government agents, and charcoal making became a difficult occupation. It also became unprofitable because gas and oil gained popularity as domestic fuels.

Certain traditional occupations were also losing importance, for example, herb doctors and magicians. In 1964 only one magician remained, albeit with a practice and reputation that attracted patients not only from Tepoztlán but from nearby communities as well. One source of employment had practically dried up: farm work in the United States. Tepoztlán, like Mitla, sent some of its laborers to work in the United States, but in 1964 this had come to almost a complete stop. While it lasted, this employment provided many benefits. Some men came back to Tepoztlán with new ideas; others were able to put their savings into new businesses, new homes, land, cattle, home appliances, etc.[50]

To sum up the changes in the employment situation, it

50. Ibid., pp. 97-98. Lewis gives an account of the ways in which these laborers used their savings on their return to Tepoztlán.

may be noted that Tepoztlán seemed to have jobs for most
of its labor force. However, some seasonal unemployment
prevailed. It was reported that during some months there
were several people unemployed. Furthermore, many of those
who went to look for jobs in Cuernavaca or Mexico City
were forced to do so by the land scarcity or by the job scarcity.
They escaped unemployment by moving away from the village, but had jobs been available they would have chosen
to remain.

Before bringing this part of the study to its conclusion, a
word may be added about the role of the local governments.
On the whole, their organization and functions had not—
with the possible exception of Chan Kom—undergone noticeable changes. As in the thirties, the government officials frequently took the initiative in planning and carrying out public improvements. The most important men still tended to
hold public office and as a rule, after leaving their posts,
continued to exercise some leadership. In the smaller villages,
namely, Chan Kom and Soteapan, where with the exception
of the municipal secretary officials were paid only token
sums and where the extent of both state and federal taxation was minimal, the municipal treasuries were able to
accumulate relatively large sums which helped to pay for
the public improvements.

The contributions that the people made toward the support of the government were in some cases recognized as
taxes but not in others. What took place in Chan Kom can
serve as an illustration. Sums paid to the state government
were thought of as taxes, but sums paid to the municipality—
or the communal labor contributed to it—were not thought
so, probably because the money stayed in the community.
The former were disliked and resented; the latter were
accepted.

In all the villages the taxes collected by the state government were (1) real estate taxes and (2) business taxes, and in the main both tended to be relatively low. In Chan Kom only the commercial establishments paid state taxes, and for a village store they could run from 50 to around 100 pesos a year.[51] In Mitla and Tepoztlán, on a per capita basis the taxes annually paid to the state were somewhat lower, seemingly in the range of 20 to 75 pesos.[52]

The local assessments and contributions were much higher. To begin with there was communal labor. In Chan Kom civil duty—consisting mainly of police work and of keeping guard at the municipal building—required two weeks of a man's time every year. But then there were the special projects, which could easily require another two weeks on the average. Hence, in communal labor alone, on the basis of a six-day week and four weeks of service, a man contributed around 240 pesos a year[53] to the support of the local government. Most of the time contributed, moreover, had an opportunity cost. Had a man not been engaged in communal labor he would have been working on his cornfield or looking after his cattle. It is likely that more communal work was performed during

51. Table 21 (chap. 5) shows the taxes paid by two of Chan Kom's commercial establishments. For data on the taxes paid by the people of the other villages see tables 16, 26, and 31 (all in chap. 5). It may be noted that in Tepoztlán and Mitla the combined real estate-mercantile tax could reach 200 pesos or more.

52. This range applies to 1963 and tends to be confirmed by census data for the state of Morelos—where Tepoztlán is located—for 1956. These data show that the 1956 state income from taxes and various duties amounted to 11,808,167 pesos. Given a state population of 307,581, it can be found that the per capita state tax amounted to 38 pesos. Taking price changes into account, the 1963 range of 20 to 75 pesos seems reasonable. These data are from *Estado de Morelos, obras y servicios públicos* (Mexico: Banco National Hipotecario Urbano y de obras públicas, 1961), pp. 8, 16, and app. 1.

53. This figure is arrived at by using the official minimum wage for farm laborers in the state of Yucatán. For 1964-65 this wage had been set by the federal government at 14 pesos per day, but assuming a conservative rate of 10 pesos per day for Chan Kom in 1963, the weekly minimum wage would have been 60 pesos. In 1963 the actual wage for farm laborers in Tepoztlán varied from 10 to 12 pesos per day. For the 1964-65 official farm and nonfarm minimum wages for the different regions of the country see *Anuario estadístico 1962-1963* (Mexico: Dirección General de Estadística, 1965), pp. 314-16.

the off season, but it does not seem that this was the case at all times.[54]

In addition to communal labor there were the assessments for special projects, the municipal taxes themselves, and special contributions that the people made in money or in kind. These payments are more difficult to estimate because the projects varied from year to year and because the funds collected in one year were sometimes spent in another. Thus the cost of the municipal building in Soteapan, excluding communal labor and special contributions, amounted to 72,000 pesos, which divided by a village population of some 1,600 persons represented a per capita levy of 45 pesos. However, in this case the funds were accumulated over a number of years by assessments on businesses and probably included some contributions from other communities in the municipality. An annual sum of 20 pesos per capita is probably a reasonable estimate of the amount contributed in money and in kind for special public projects.[55]

The municipal taxes tended to be rather low. They were levied on businesses for the most part and included such items as taxes for the use of the marketplace, special taxes for the schools, taxes on cattle slaughtered, etc.[56] In addition the municipal income was supplemented by various fees, fines, and other less important revenues. Even with this supple-

54. The work on the road that the author witnessed was carried out in late March and early April, months during which the burning and preparation of the bush take place. Thus the villagers had their own work to do, and some of them actually divided their day between work on the road and work on their fields or businesses (store owners were also doing communal work).
55. It may be recalled that in Tepoztlán donations of money, materials, and labor were made not only for village-wide projects but also for neighborhood projects and that when work on the water system started in the late forties each household was assessed 20 pesos. For the electrification of the village the assessment was 100 pesos, but some families paid this sum gradually. Chan Kom's assessment for the school and for the electrification project was 10 pesos per adult male in each case. In short, an average per capita contribution for special public projects of 20 pesos a year looks like a reasonable amount.
56. See pp. 54-55 for some of the taxes charged in the base period.

mental income, however, the amounts collected on a per capita basis were small, probably on the order of 10 pesos a year.[57] In Chan Kom the total municipal income was around 5,000 pesos, which divided by a population of 386 yielded about 13 pesos per person each year. However, it probably included some small sums contributed by a few municipal settlements.[58] In any event, a per capita municipal tax of 10 pesos a year seems plausible.

Putting these various taxes and contributions together, it seems that an effective per capita tax of around 308 pesos was paid by the villagers, the largest portion being introduced of course by the value of the communal labor.[59] If this figure is related to the per capita income of the villages, it can be seen that in 1963 it represented better than 17 percent of per capita income.[60] This was not a small percentage by any means, particularly if it is considered that for the country in 1965 taxes represented 9.1 percent of GNP.[61]

One problem seemed to be emerging in Tepoztlán, the largest village, and it was a decline in the use of communal

---

57. According to the publication of the Banco Nacional Hipotecario Urbano y de Obras Públicas (see n. 52 above), in the state of Morelos the average income (from all sources) of a municipality the size of Tepoztlán amounted to 6.72 pesos per capita, but this was for 1950. Yates mentions that for 1958 the small municipalities had a municipal income of 5 pesos per capita, or less. See P. L. Yates, *El desarrollo regional de Mexico* (Mexico: Banco de Mexico, 1961), p. 193.

58. Soteapan, which had the Mexican petroleum company as one of its taxpayers, had in all likelihood a larger municipal income. It may be recalled that Foster estimated that in 1941 its municipal income was around 2,000 pesos.

59. The breakdown of the figure is the following: communal labor, 240 pesos; state tax, 38 pesos; assessments and contributions for special projects, 20 pesos; municipal taxes, 10 pesos. It should be added that in Mitla and Tepoztlán one more tax was beginning to be collected: federal income tax.

60. See third column of table 32 in chap. 5. The percentage is arrived at by dividing 308 pesos by the average per capita income for all the villages (1,526 pesos) after adding to this figure the imputation for communal labor (240 pesos) since the latter did not enter into the reckoning of the per capita incomes shown by table 32.

61. See A. N. Navarrete, "Mexico: Su progreso economico y social," *El mercado de valores* (Mexico) 12 June 1967, p. 503.

labor.[62] Given the latter's importance, this could become serious if the trend continued. It would mean that as communal labor declined, to maintain the same level of activity in the public sector, it would eventually be necessary to pay for labor that had previously been obtained free.

62. During the author's visit to Tepoztlán a hoe agriculturist accidentally started a fire on one of the mountains. On the first day "volunteers" were recruited to put it out, but the brigade so organized was rather small and the fire continued. On subsequent days it become more and more difficult to find volunteer fire fighters, and the mountain burned for a week.

4

On the Verge of
Commercialized Agriculture

The agricultural progress of the villages over three decades is reviewed in this chapter. By way of introduction attention may be called to the dual nature of agriculture in Mexico. First, there is a modern sector comprising the irrigated lands which, until a few years ago, were located in the northern and northwestern part of the country. This sector is characterized by such features as large ejido and private holdings, the use of tractors and other mechanized equipment, crop rotation, and use of fertilizers. Needless to say, it is this sector that has produced most of the extraordinary increases in the nation's agricultural output. But there is also a primitive sector of marginal lands that lack irrigation and which therefore must depend on seasonal rain. Generally speaking, in this sector there is no mechanization or modern implements, fragmented holdings are the rule, the cultivation of corn predominates, and the use of fertilizers and crop rotation is only beginning. Obviously in the thirties the agriculture of the villages was of the primitive type. Their situation in 1964 was the following.

In Soteapan coffee growing had received increasing attention. Most peasants also continued to grow corn. Beans, pineapples, bananas, and sugar cane were still planted. The methods and the tools employed did not seem to have undergone noticeable improvements; slash-and-burn agriculture still prevailed. Mountain streams were still supplying the village with water, and the cropland was still dependent on seasonal rain.

Until 1960 Soteapan had been the only village of the four not affected by the agrarian reform. In that year the allocation of ejido lands began, and in 1964 the various communities were still in the process of taking possession of them. The new allocations had affected many farmers. Some had to give up not only some of their cornfields but also lands which they had planted with fruit trees and coffee. Hence, in 1964 the agricultural situation was in a state of rapid change, and many farmers, uncertain as to what the final settlements were going to be, had been cultivating less than their customary amount of land.

In general, changes in agriculture had been slow and various factors tended to retard agricultural development. Among these the following could be singled out: (1) the isolation of Soteapan and the resulting limited exposure to better outside methods; (2) the fact that the export crop (coffee) could be grown profitably without mechanized equipment and so there had been no pressing need to introduce new methods; and (3) a psychological factor that seemed to have exerted a negative influence. This factor had manifested itself mainly as envy and resentment, especially when one of the villagers achieved some material success. A number of cases were reported to the author of individuals who through the years invested their savings in cattle and who would have become successful cattle breeders except for the resentment of others. Whenever their herds grew, envious individuals appeared and either shot the animals, hung them, or else destroyed the fences around cornfields and plantations so that the cattle could enter and eat the crops, thus provoking the retaliatory action of the landowners. Envy had also been the motivation behind the burning of sugarcane fields that belonged to more successful farmers. To complicate the situation, there had been a tradition of violence in the region, and envy had caused at times not only destruction of property but death or injury to persons. Under such conditions the prudent man had to be careful not to become too successful.

The villagers of Chan Kom, on the contrary, admired success and individual initiative, and the acquisition and profitable use of wealth were actively pursued by all. The people have tended to lead peaceful lives, and acts of violence, even though they have occurred, have been rare. Like Soteapan, Chan Kom has not had noticeable improvements in agriculture; however, as was explained in chapter 2, improved methods are limited in large measure by the nature of the soil. In 1964 the supply of land was still adequate, one reason being that on two occasions the local leaders were careful to request, and obtain, additional ejido grants. Thanks to this policy and to the loss of population caused by the religious conflict, the man-land ratio was better in 1964 than in 1930.[1] Hence, even though the slash-and-burn technique continued in use, there was still no problem of land scarcity and a man planted as much land as he wanted to. In practice most men limited the size of their plots to from four to eight hectares, although in 1963 two men cultivated about sixteen hectares each.

As in the past, corn continued to be the principal crop. A surplus was usually produced which was exported by truck to either Mérida or Valladolid. The ability of the people to grow corn in excess of their needs had proven to be a blessing in times of distress. In 1942–44, for example, the region was hit by drought and a plague of locusts, and many villages were hard struck by food shortages.[2] Chan Kom, by importing flour for bread from Mérida and by drawing from its supply of corn, was able to feed not only its own population but that of neighboring settlements as well.

In 1964 beans were the second most important crop and they were also exported. Other crops tended to be consumed locally; among these in 1963 were squash, sweet potatoes, hot peppers, lentils, various root crops, and a number of fruits—

1. In 1930 Chan Kom had fifty-four agriculturalists and a common ejido of 2,400 ha., or 44.4 ha. per agriculturalist. In the spring of 1964 the size of the ejido had gone up to 5,703 ha., and there were less than one hundred agriculturalists, i.e., each one of them had a minimum of 57 ha.
2. Redfield, *A Village That Chose Progress*, pp. 20, 69, 151.

including hog plums, papaya, limes, lemons, oranges, and bananas. Even though land had continued to be plentiful, its productivity seemed to have declined during the thirties and forties. Redfield found that in 1931 the average corn yield per hectare during the first year after burning was 840 kilograms; in 1948, however, the yield had been reduced to 525 kilograms.[3] In 1963 it was around 500 kilograms per hectare. No studies have been made to determine the cause of the decline. Redfield thought that an accelerated land use, accompanied by a more rapid destruction of large trees and by soil erosion, may have been contributing factors. It may also be that the growing herds roaming about the countryside prevent the bush from developing to its full potential, and therefore the amount of nutrients obtained from its burning is not as large as in past years.

Henequen is the great export product of Yucatán, but its cultivation in Chan Kom was restricted to the backyards of a few houses, where it seemed to thrive. Unfortunately, nobody had seriously attempted its exploitation and perhaps this was just as well because its production is subject to many regulations. There are producing and marketing cooperatives that control its movement to market and that make it difficult for the small grower to enter the field.

As aforementioned, improvements in agriculture had been nil, but in the early fifties some of the old farmers tried to erect barb wire fences around their fields. Since originally all the land constituted the village's ejido and private property rights had not been clearly understood, there were some persons who protested the erection of the fences and others who went as far as to cut the wires. As a result there were no further attempts to erect fences until 1963 when two individuals put them up again. At the time of the author's visit the fences were still standing. One of these individuals, Mr. Ceme, had been interested in introducing some innovations,

3. Ibid., p. 55.

one of which was to dig a well and install a gasoline-operated water pump. With this equipment he was irrigating a piece of land planted with a grass that he used as fodder for his cattle.

Mitla was affected by the agrarian reform shortly after Parson's last visit. Two haciendas were expropriated and 885 hectares were taken from them. This land plus additional grants gave Mitla some 7,470 hectares, exclusive of the area where the village is located. Most of the land is mountainous and depends on seasonal rain; only 20 percent of it is considered tillable. When the land was redistributed, consideration was given to its quality, which resulted in some peasants receiving only one-half hectare while others received as much as six hectares. In 1964 there were 300 villagers holding ejido grants; unfortunately, some holdings were located on rugged mountain slopes that allowed nothing better than digging stick agriculture. Similar mountain slopes were being used by those who owned no land.

Corn was still Mitla's most important crop. The amount produced varied from year to year depending on rainfall. In 1963—a year with poor rainfall—the average corn yield for the municipality was 571 kilograms per hectare, but the yield varied sharply from one type of land to another.[4] Land close to the streams, which contained moisture and therefore did not depend entirely on rain, produced 1,500 kilograms of corn per hectare whereas land that used rainfall exclusively produced only 300 kilograms per hectare. Land that had lost its fertility was being left fallow for one year.

---

4. All the municipalities in Mexico are required by the federal government to submit annual reports on agricultural yields and on production of crops, livestock, poultry, and fruits. These data show at times marked inconsistencies; nevertheless the 1963 data quoted (which were obtained from the annual report) are approximately correct. Compared to those of other years the yield is low because the 1963 rainfall was below average. In 1960, a year with good rainfall, the reported average corn yield was 1,067 kg. per ha. The 1963 yield, as determined by the author, was 537 kg. per ha.

As far as new methods are concerned, in 1964 some peasants were becoming acquainted with fertilizers, although their use was still limited. One reason for this seemed to be that the purchase of fertilizers is a losing proposition if the rains fail, since fertilizer can do little without water. It is true that if in a time of drought the fertilizer remains on the soil for one year, it does not lose all its potency. However, what the peasant would see in that particular year is both the loss of the crop and the loss of the money invested in fertilizer.

The use of the wooden plow was still prevalent in 1964, and some farmers were also using steel plows; but Mitla already had a farmer who owned a tractor, and there were about twelve others who had dug wells and installed gasoline-operated water pumps to irrigate their lands. One of the farmers had tried an experiment with amazing results. He planted corn on a piece of land that apparently had become unproductive. He used ordinary seed and no fertilizer but pumped water from one of the streams. The amount of corn that he produced was three times greater than what he had produced on it previously. Furthermore, he thought that by using fertilizer and hybrid seed, production could be increased fivefold.

Beans were also planted in Mitla in the agricultural year 1963, but they were attacked by pests and the output was negligible. In the poorer lands century plants, which require neither good soil nor much water, were being grown,[5] and a

5. The cultivation of century plants appears profitable although it requires time, and probably for this reason the average peasant does not use his land for this purpose. The century plants grown in Mitla are used to make an alcoholic beverage and need six years to grow. When fully grown they sell for from 15 to 20 pesos each. In one hectare of land the number of plants that can be grown varies of course with the nature of the soil; in that of medium quality 1,300 plants can be planted. If they are sold at 15 pesos, they bring in a total of 19,500 pesos which prorated can give a man an annual income of 3,250 pesos. The same hectare of land planted with corn (assuming that it produces the average 537 kg.), with the price of corn between 0.85 and 1.10 pesos per kg., produces a much smaller annual income.

few farmers grew castor-oil plants. Alfalfa, chickpeas, and various fruits were also grown in 1963.

As in the past, some families owned livestock, poultry, hogs, goats, or sheep. Some farmers owned oxen, which they kept for their own use or for hire—charging from twenty-five to thirty pesos per day. Since the weaving of woolen shawls was increasing in importance, the breeding of sheep also received more attention. All the wool locally produced was finding a convenient market within the village itself.

Agriculture in Tepoztlán, at the time of Lewis's second visit in 1956, seemed to have undergone only some minor changes. At one time the export of hog plums became an important source of income, but a black fly had damaged the trees and whatever hog plums were being produced were intended mainly for home consumption. Low prices had also contributed to the curtailment of hog plum production. Just as Chan Kom's farmers curtailed corn production when the price of corn was low, so did the growers of hog plums in Tepoztlán when hog plum prices declined.

Lewis noted that there had been an increase in the number of nonagricultural occupations and that many people were making a living outside agriculture, but in agriculture there was still no mechanization and no introduction of new crops.[6] He added, however, that some farmers were already using commercial fertilizer and that two or three gladiola farms had been established. As later developments have shown, both of the latter events have been part of a remarkable series of innovations—particularly since the late fifties —which have amounted to nothing less than an agricultural transformation.

In Tepoztlán in 1964 tractors were employed; the use of commercial fertilizers and of various types of manure had

6. O. Lewis, *Tepoztlán*, pp. 96-97.

become widespread; new crops had been introduced on a commercial scale; crop rotation, insecticides, and fumigation of plants were in use, and farmers had access to information and supervisory services provided by both the state and the federal governments. Moreover, these changes had occurred in a period of less than a decade.

The number of tractors in use in Tepoztlán in the spring of 1964 was twelve and the number of owners was ten. The funds to purchase these tractors came from savings, profits from agriculture, loans, and the proceeds from sales of land and cattle. The ownership of large tracts had not been a prerequisite to the purchase of a tractor. Most of the men who owned them did not have large landholdings, but they had found two practices that helped make the purchase of a tractor profitable. First, they tried to increase the size of their landholdings by renting land from others, and second, they worked other people's lands, charging from twelve to fifteen pesos per 1,000 square meters of plowed land. The use of tractors had been gaining in popularity, mainly because most farmers were able to increase their yields. As a result, according to some farmers, the use of plow and oxen had been declining. Furthermore, a man who paid for the services of a tractor tried to maximize the return on his expenditure, and so instead of cultivating corn only, he shifted to the new and more profitable crops.

The use of commercial fertilizers had spread considerably. It was reported that even peasants who still practiced hoe culture had begun to use them. A store had been opened which in addition to selling fertilizers tried to give advice on how and which type to use. At the same time manure (particularly chicken manure) was being used as fertilizer and had become a marketable product.[7]

The most important new crops were: tomatoes, squash,

7. The supply of chicken manure was increased in the late fifties when a number of chicken farms were started—one of them by a former YMCA trainee who was using modern methods and high quality chickens.

gladiolas, and watermelons. Tomatoes and squash had been grown in the village for a long time, but not until the sixties had they been grown by modern methods and on a commercial scale. Formerly there were some persons who grew tomatoes, but these were of poor quality and were intended mainly for family consumption.

It is difficult to find a single cause that may account for the introduction of the new crops and for the modernization of agriculture in general because there have been several contributing factors. Among them the following four seem to be the principal ones: the training and agricultural experimentation which the YMCA carried out, the aid and consultation services that the federal and the state governments made available to farmers, the influence exerted by former farm laborers who worked in the United States, and finally, the presence of outsiders who appeared at critical moments and actually initiated the cultivation of new crops on a large scale.

The last of the above-mentioned factors played an important role in the introduction of gladiolas, which were first grown on a commercial scale by a Spaniard who arrived in the village a few years ago. This man rented land and hired a few Tepoztecans to work for him as laborers. The venture turned out to be a profitable one, but once they had learned the new art, the hired hands began to leave his employment in order to grow gladiolas on their own. Others in turn learned from these few, and thus the cultivation of gladiolas spread not only throughout Tepoztlán but to nearby villages as well.

In similar fashion, the growing of tomatoes was sparked by the work of an Italian in a village some thirty kilometers away. He started out in a manner similar to that of the Spaniard, and in no time profits amply rewarded his efforts. As in the previous case, the men who had worked for him and whose lands he had rented soon learned the art, and after two or three years they refused to renew the leases. Then they went into business for themselves. It was not long before some of them were able to buy their own tractors and trucks. News of their success reached Tepoztlán and the interest of a few men was aroused. In time some Tepoztecans went to work for the tomato growers, learned from them, and then returned to Tepoztlán to start growing tomatoes on their own. Eventually they became successful and were able to purchase their own mechanized equipment.

The growing of watermelons although not as widespread as tomato growing, was another new crop. In this instance the interest of the Tepoztecan farmers was aroused by the success which a government-operated experimental station had with them. Some men decided to try cultivating watermelons and received free instruction and special advice from the station. In 1964 watermelons were grown by a few farmers, usually in addition to other crops.

Squash was another agricultural product of recent introduction. Like the other three new crops mentioned, it had also become a cash crop, and thousands of boxes were being exported—mainly to Mexico City.

The practice of rotating crops had also made its appearance in Tepoztlán and some farmers were shifting from the cultivation of one crop to that of another. Corn was still widely grown but its preponderence seemed to be disappearing.[8] The new crops, moreover, were grown not only by the younger and more enterprising farmers but also by old-timers who never had grown anything but corn and beans. Even these two traditional crops had benefited from the modernization process; fertilizers and mechanization had improved their yields.

All this progress had not been achieved without difficulties.

8. Tradition and nonpecuniary motives, however, die hard. The author asked one of the successful tomato growers why he continued to grow corn when his earnings from tomatoes were so much greater: "Because the growing of corn is so beautiful," he replied. A second farmer gave as his reason the fact that he enjoyed eating fresh corn-on-the-cob roasted unshelled on an open fire. Another farmer explained that corn provided the means of spreading his risk because at times the price of tomatoes fluctuated widely.

One serious problem had been the appearance of pests that damaged the crops. To correct this problem a number of measures had been taken. One of them—still prevalent in 1964—was to seek the consultation of government agronomists. These specialists came to the village, without charge, to make investigations on the spot, to give lectures on pest control and the use of fertilizers, or to teach farmers the best methods of growing a given crop. In this manner many farmers had learned fumigation and were using it on their crops. Some pest-control projects had been undertaken which affected the whole region. In 1964 a pest-control experiment involving the breeding of special types of bacteria was in progress, and some Tepoztecan farmers had offered to cooperate.

The state government has occasionally sponsored various special programs. In 1953, for instance, it tried to interest farmers in growing olive trees and to this end sold a quantity of the trees for the nominal sum of one peso each. Some Tepoztecans bought them and after planting them were visited by an agronomist whose purpose was to extend any help or advice that might be required. Since it takes a minimum of about fifteen years before they start producing, in 1964 it was still too early to know whether the experiment was going to be successful.

Two old agricultural problems, land and water scarcity, had remained unsolved. After mechanization was introduced, some farmers discovered that there are some lands that can be cultivated after the rainy season. The soil conserves enough moisture so that if a tractor is used for plowing, crops can be grown without rain. Unfortunately, these same lands cannot be cultivated during the rainy season because they often become flooded. Nevertheless some farmers had begun to dig water wells to provide some irrigation. They hoped that by supplementing the moisture left by the rains they would be able to obtain not only better crops but two crops a year. Another type of irrigation had been introduced by some farmers who own orchards. In this instance small water reservoirs had been built which are filled during the rainy season; later in the year, as the trees need it, water is drawn with buckets to irrigate them. On the whole, irrigation projects had been few and most crops continued to depend on seasonal rain.

The problem of land scarcity had been made more acute by the population increase and by the purchases of land by outsiders. The ejido authorities stated that during the last few years they had been unable to satisfy the many requests for land that they received. Consequently, there were still men in Tepoztlán who had no other way to make a living except by hoe culture on the mountain slopes. Among Tepoztecans themselves the ownership of large tracts did not seem prevalent. The official records showed one man owning various plots that added up to some twenty-six hectares, but even the reputed large landholders or the men who had purchased tractors did not own more than from eight to fourteen hectares of land of all types.[9]

To conclude this review of the agricultural changes, it may be added that besides the crops already mentioned Tepoztlán had continued to produce various fruits. Most families were still raising poultry, and there were some individuals who bred hogs. Others were breeding cattle, the quality of which had shown some improvement. Then, there were some persons who sold milk, and they in particular had made efforts to improve the quality of their herds.

In his first study of Tepoztlán, Lewis examined the degree of inequality in the ownership of wealth.[10] One of his conclusions was that there was a trend toward the concentration of wealth, particularly in the case of land. He found that 4 percent of the families owned about 25 percent of the land

9. A man was found who owned three pieces of land of varying quality which added up to 19.5 ha. He grew corn (for family consumption), squash, and tomatoes. His farming equipment included two tractors and two trucks. At the peak of his season he was employing from ten to twelve agricultural workers.
10. O. Lewis, *Life in a Mexican Village,* pp. 174.

and that a similar pattern existed in the ownership of cattle. In his second study, however, he noted that what he had previously classified as the "middle economic group" had doubled in size and had come to encompass 25 percent of the population.[11] In his view this group (which included professionals, white-collar workers, self-employed artisans, and shopkeepers) was beginning to constitute a true middle class. On the other hand, the lower economic group, while it had become relatively smaller, still included the majority— around 65 percent—of the population. According to him, inflation and the prohibition of charcoal production had made this group even poorer.

Between the time of Lewis's second investigation in 1956 and the author's 1964 survey, so many changes had taken place that without probing at some length, it seemed difficult to determine what the 1964 situation was concerning wealth inequality and, more important perhaps, income inequality. Some income differentials—for instance, between a successful new-crop grower and a hoe-type agriculturalist—had undoubtedly become more pronounced. In the absence of data, however, it did not seem possible to determine what shifts had taken place in the relative standings of the different income groups.

In conclusion, there can be little question that by 1964 Tepoztlán had witnessed a striking agricultural transformation. The introduction of tractors, trucks, fertilizers, insecticides, crop rotation, and new cash crops could not but indicate that Tepoztlán was on the verge of commercialized agriculture. Following a similar path, Mitla was beginning to initiate the modernization of agriculture, albeit on a more modest scale. The other two communities were still very much part of the traditional agricultural sector. In them only a very limited amount of innovation had occurred, and the cultivation of corn had maintained its supremacy.

11. O. Lewis, *Tepoztlán,* pp. 102-3.

What is the significance of the agricultural changes, and what are the prospects for the villages in agriculture? These questions will be examined in the concluding chapter; in the next some information is presented about the state of village households at the time of the terminal survey.

5

A Survey
of Rural Households

In this chapter the focus is shifted from the village to the household level. This has a twofold purpose: first, additional data can be presented that will contribute toward a better understanding of the economic situation of the villages in the terminal period; and second, these data will aid in the analysis of the changes recorded in the two preceding chapters.

Before the data are presented a word may be inserted at this point concerning their nature. The data relating to households were obtained through interviews conducted by the author at the time of his visit to the villages in the spring of 1964. They are based on factual experience, but they are offered as nothing more than reasonable estimates. The informants were asked to answer a number of questions concerning their economic activities in 1963, but no attempt was made to confirm the veracity of their answers nor were return visits made to determine the consistency of the replies. In spite of these shortcomings it does not seem that the answers suffer from rank inaccuracies, and within the context of all the information gathered they do not present inconsistencies or raise doubts so serious as to invalidate their usefulness.

Accuracy in a survey of rural households such as the present one is difficult to attain because the village people do not keep records of such things as income and expenditures; hence in many instances the respondents simply could not reply. There were some, for example, who did not know the value of their houses or of their lands—probably because sales of this type were not a common occurrence. Consequently, to correct this deficiency, estimates were obtained from others who owned similar houses or who were able to make an educated guess.

A random and larger sample of households would have been desirable; in the present case it was only possible to obtain information from a limited number of persons who, overcoming their reluctance and distrust, agreed to answer the questions. The replies were at times evasive or vague, and for this reason some items in the tables that follow appear as unknown. Some persons were interviewed who, although amused at being the subject of an economic inquiry, lacked so much knowledge of their affairs that whatever information they gave proved to be of little value. From a few persons no cooperation whatever was obtained.

Some of the men who had become prosperous in the last few years did not talk freely; it seemed as though they felt the need to maintain secrecy about their operations. Then there were others who feared that some disclosures could later be used to their disadvantage—for taxation purposes, for example. Consequently, both income and assets tended to be understated. In Tepoztlán, where it was reported that there was a tax on livestock of five pesos per head, not many farmers were willing to disclose the exact size of their herds, and much the same thing happened regarding disclosures on the production of various fruits.

The tables that follow summarize the data collected in the interviews. They cover different economic activities of the households and are presented for each village in the order visited. The first of these table gives a few general characteristics of the households sampled in Mitla.

On the basis of the data of table 12, Mitla's average household in 1964 consisted of 5.5 persons. The majority of the

TABLE 12

General Characteristics of Households Sampled in Mitla, 1963

HOUSE-HOLD NUMBER	NUMBER OF PERSONS	NUMBER OF EARNERS	MAIN AND SECONDARY OCCUPATION OF HEAD	HIGHEST SCHOOL GRADE OF HEAD	AGE OF HEAD	ECONOMIC LEVEL OF HOUSE-HOLD[a]
1	6	2	Farmer, shawl maker	5	42	M
2	6	1	Farmer, basket maker	1	45	L
3	11	3	Mason	5	40	H
4	2	2	Farmer, merchant	4	72	H
5	4	1	Farmer, real estate owner	0	73	H
6	4	1	Farmer, shawl maker	4	34	L
7	4	2	Farmer, laborer	0	42	L
8	7	2	Farmer, travel merchant	0	68	L

[a] High, medium, or low. Level based on the general regard in which the household was held and on assets and income.

households had more than one earner, and with only one exception (household 3), no household was headed by a man who made a living from agriculture exclusively. The level of education attained by the heads of household tended to be rather low. In two cases (households 7 and 8), lack of education was associated with low economic condition. However, the head of household 5 never went to school and yet of the heads of household sampled, he was the wealthiest (although not the wealthiest man in Mitla). The average age of the heads of household was 52. Contrary to what might be expected, in Mitla, and in the other villages as well, men of advanced age were found actively heading their households and still engaging in full-time work.

On the basis of the data it is difficult to establish whether age was directly related to economic level. Wealthy men were found who were relatively young (household 3), and old men were found who were rather poor (household 8). However, in two instances (households 4 and 5), wealth was clearly associated with old age. Table 13 shows that the majority of the households owned various assets, so the "low" economic category shown by the last column of table 12 is not synonymous with destitution. On the basis of income and wealth, "really poor" households seemed to be the exception rather than the rule.

The head of household 8 had been a resident of Mitla for twenty-seven years but all the others were natives. The fathers of all the heads of households had been farmers, although in some cases they had also been part-time traveling merchants. Asked to compare their present with their past economic condition, the respondents tended to state that their 1964 economic condition was better. Occasionally some men offered different opinions. The head of household 2 said that he had seen no change during the recent past; the head of household 3 said that past years had been good and bad; and the head of household 4 had mixed feelings because in addition to health problems he had had a small liquor distillery put out of business by high state taxes. The head of household 7 thought that the time prior to the agrarian reform had been better because his father had had steady work in the hacienda as a sharecropper. To him this had been a satisfactory arrangement even though sharecroppers had to turn over one-fifth of their crops to the owner. In 1964 this man owned very poor land and for him 1963 had been a particularly bad year; so he had reason to be pessimistic. Lastly, the head of household 8 considered the remote past better because his crops in the preceding five years had been bad. Asked to state what their prospects were for the future, most respondents expressed optimism; however, the heads of household 3 and 6 said that their prospects were uncertain, and the head of household 8 stated that he foresaw no change from his then current condition.

Turning next to the subject of family wealth, table 13 presents information about the most important assets owned by eight Mitla households. The first thing to be noted is that all the households owned the houses in which they lived. All the houses were masonry structures made either of ordi-

TABLE 13

Principal Assets Owned by Households

Sampled in Mitla, 1963

(Current Market Value in Pesos)

HOUSE-HOLD NUMBER	HOUSE	LAND[a]	ANIMALS[b]	TOOLS	PRODUCTION GOODS	DURABLES[c]	OTHER	TOTAL VALUE[d]
1	6,000	3.00[e]	330	200	undet.[f]	1,050	undet.	7,580
2	5,000	1.50[e]	730	250	. . . .	250	. . . .	6,230
		1.00[g]						
3	15,000	. . . .	. . . .	2,000	. . . .	1,200	. . . .	18,200
4	10,000	13.00[g]	undet.	undet.	2,700[h]	750	undet.	19,950
					6,500[i]			
5	50,000	13.00[g]	4,000	500	18,200[i]	1,950	120,000[j]	194,650
					undet.[h]			
6	3,300[k]	2.00[g]	1,220	520	1,300[l]	. . . .	. . . .	6,340
7	5,500	2.00[e]	220	150	400[m]	250	. . . .	6,520
8	4,000	3.00[e]	260	500	1,800[l]	1,200	. . . .	8,960
		0.75[g]			1,200[m]			

[a] Hectares of land cultivated.
[b] Figures include the average village price of chickens (22 pesos), turkeys (60 pesos), and hogs (600 pesos).
[c] Figures include the average village price of sewing machines (800 pesos), radios (250 pesos), bicycles (400 pesos), and typewriters (500 pesos).
[d] Excludes value of cultivated land except for household 5.
[e] Size of ejido holdings.
[f] Looms (value undetermined).
[g] Size of private land holdings.
[h] Construction cost (undetermined for no. 5) of water wells used for irrigation.
[i] Purchase price of water pumps.
[j] Of this sum, 105,000 pesos represent ownership of real estate (including value of cultivated land) and 15,000 pesos represent the value of life insurance policies.
[k] Value of prorated share of property.
[l] Value of oxen—on the basis of a price of 1,300-1,800 pesos per team.
[m] Value of burros—on the basis of an average price of 200 pesos.

nary bricks or of adobes. All had adjacent plots as well as storage facilities for grain either as part of the house or as separate outside granaries. The heads of households 2 and 7 worked in the United States as farm laborers and with their savings built their houses in 1946. Similarly, the son of the head of household 8 also worked in the United States, and he contributed toward the construction of the house, which had been built in stages. As savings accumulated they were used to purchase construction materials and to pay the wages of a mason.

With the exception of households 4 and 5 (both headed by old and wealthy men who owned relatively large plots of land with irrigation facilities), the landholdings of the other households consisted of small plots—ejido, private, or both—of poor quality and unirrigated. Only one head of a household (6) cultivated land on half-shares and this involved a small one-hectare plot. The head of household 7, as indicated above, owned very poor land, and his crops were frequently quite meager. He made no efforts to improve his land, mostly because he had become discouraged by a continuing series of setbacks. But, each year he mustered enough hope and went back to the land despite his feeling that another setback might be in store. The value of land was difficult to ascertain, particularly in view of the quasi-ownership of ejido holdings; consequently, land value does not enter into the total value of the assets shown in the last column of the table.

Ownership of animals was widespread, especially of poultry which not only was part of the diet but provided a source of income. Several households also owned production goods other than tools. These consisted of looms, irrigation wells, water pumps, pack animals, and oxen. The ownership of durables was also widespread and included two popular items; sewing machines and radios. Bicycles were owned by households with young people and two households owned typewriters. In several cases, for households 1 and 4, an asset was possessed, but its value was undetermined. Represented as "other" assets on the table, household 1 owned an inventory of wool, dyes, and finished woolen shawls, and household 4 owned some distillery equipment and the furnishings and stock of a small retail liquor store.

The large total value of the assets of household 5 merits some explanation. As indicated previously, this household was headed by one of the wealthy men of the village. This man never went to school but taught himself to read and write. Some of his friends remembered that in 1928 he made a living as peddler and mule driver. He had also been a musician; but in this occupation he received no compensation other than food and liquor, and the latter had lead him into heavy drinking. In the twenties the only assets in his possession consisted of a modest house which his wife had inherited, but he did not remain poor for long. As the years went by he found the road to success in commerce, agriculture, and real estate, and in 1964 he was one of Mitla's wealthy.

The last column of the table understates the true asset values because the price of land, as already indicated, is not included. Furthermore, two other important items are also missing: the value of jewelry and cash on hand. The ownership of the first was not unusual, and so far as the second is concerned, Redfield and others found that peasants kept money in tin cans lying around the house or else buried on some part of the house lot.

Next to be examined is the income of the households and the most important income sources (table 14). The second column of the table shows that the production of corn was common to practically all the households. Unfortunately, in most cases the amount produced did not seem large enough to take care of the household needs. A family of six consumed from 3 to 4 kilograms of corn per day and in addition

TABLE 14

Annual Income, by Principal Sources, of Households

Sampled in Mitla, 1963

(In Current Pesos)

HOUSE-HOLD NUMBER	CORN OUTPUT[a]	OTHER AGRICULTURAL PRODUCTS[b]	ANIMAL PRODUCTS[e]	ARTS AND CRAFTS	OTHER SOURCES	TOTAL EARNED INCOME	PER CAPITA INCOME
1	1,710	440	700	7,800[d]	3,100[e]	13,750	2,291
2	1,420	1,970[f]	....	1,030[g]	....	4,420	736
3	....	....	....	12,000[h]	3,600[e] 6,000[i]	21,600	1,963
4	7,600	undet.[j]	undet.	....	1,560[i]	9,160	4,580
5	450	15,715[k]	....	....	6,120[i]	22,285	5,571
6	950	1,450	600	925[e]	....	3,925	981
7	190	....	600	....	3,500[e]	4,290	1,072
8	1,420	205	675	....	260[e] 3,000[i]	5,560	794

[a] Based on an average price of 0.95 pesos per kg. of corn.
[b] The figures without symbols include the value of the output of corn stalks and husks (1.25 pesos per bundle), the value of the bean crop (based on an average price of 2.70 pesos per kg. of beans), and the value of the output of fruits and vegetables.
[e] Figures include the value of the production of eggs (0.40 pesos each), and the value of chickens (average price 22 pesos) and turkeys (average price 60 pesos) sold.
[d] Income from manufacture of woolen shawls.
[e] Wages.
[f] Includes corn stalk and husk production in the amount of 310 pesos and a prorated value of century plant production in the amount of 1,660 pesos.
[g] Income from manufacture of baskets.
[h] Fees and profits from housebuilding.
[i] Income from commerce.
[j] Value of alfalfa crop (amount of income undetermined).
[k] Includes the value of the output of the following items: apples (600 pesos), alfalfa (1,600 pesos), fodder (700 pesos), lemons (400 pesos), coffee (75 pesos), bananas (100 pesos), papayas (120 pesos), vegetables (200 pesos), cactus plants (260 pesos), and prorated value of century plant production (11,600 pesos).
[l] Rent.

it needed from 1 to 3 kilograms for animal feed; hence, as a minimum, some 2,000 kilograms of corn were needed by the average family per year. Two hectares of land (all the farmers sampled cultivated this much or more in 1963) if irrigated, fertilized, deeply plowed, etc., could easily have produced much more than the minimum indicated, but under the circumstances the corn crop in some cases was disappointingly low—as the figure for household 7 demonstrates.

In 1963 most Mitla farmers obtained an average corn yield of around 500 kilograms per hectare. Only two farmers reported the use of fertilizer: the head of household 5 used it occasionally on his orchards, and the head of household 6 manured his cropland every three years. The head of household 4 obtained his rather large corn crop by cultivating two good pieces of land, one with irrigation and the other with moisture drawn by seepage from one of the streams. However, he also spent 800 pesos on the cultivation of an unirrigated plot, from which the crop was only two bags of corn. Like most farmers he also planted beans, but the plants were attacked by locusts and he lost the crop—as did other farmers. To repeat, only two households (4 and 5) owned irrigated land, though it was reported that there were from ten to twelve men who had installed water pumps in their fields.

Many families were forced to buy corn every year. Households 2, 6, 7, and 8 made clear that for them it was going to be necessary to do this in 1964. The head of household 8 explained that he was in the habit of putting his own corn in storage in October (i.e., after the harvest) and that he would buy it in the village until April or May when the price would begin to rise, and then he would start to draw from his own supply.

As a rule, the corn, eggs, poultry, and home-grown vegetables produced were actually consumed by the households, but for the purpose of computing income no deductions were made from the value of total product for items directly consumed in the home. For the computation of food expenditures (see table 15) the amounts arrived at represent the value of the food consumed regardless of whether it was produced by the household or not. The same set of commodity prices was used to determine both income and expenditures.

In the case of household 4, income was earned from agricultural and animal products, but the amounts were undetermined.

Table 14 also shows how income from agriculture was supplemented with earnings from cottage industries, commerce, and wages. In fact the well-being of some households depended on this additional income. In some cases (such as that of household 1) a cottage industry could be an important source of income. The head of this household, while not considered wealthy, had turned the manufacture of woolen shawls into a profitable enterprise, and people who knew him thought that he was on his way to becoming one of Mitla's wealthy citizens.

Much variability can be seen in the last two columns of the table, which correspond to total earned income and to per capita income. The average per capita income of the eight households sampled was 1,931 pesos,[1] but it should be noted that the total earned income column does not show the true income of the households. Villagers had access to goods that were more or less freely provided by the environment, such as, firewood, construction materials, and water, not to mention the fact that the great majority of the households—including those in the sample—paid no rent. Hence the table understates the true income. A more accurate estimation would have included imputation for at least two items: expenditures on water and house rent. Had these imputations been carried out the annual income (and expenditure) of those who had water wells in their backyards or who got water from the public taps would have gone up by some 240 pesos—based on the monthly sum of 20 pesos charged to those supplied with the service—and the resulting income would have gone up still farther by an imputation for house rent ranging from 180 pesos to 1,200 pesos per year. Then, if

1. This sum is equivalent to $154 at the 1964 rate of exchange.

communal labor had also been included, the income would have gone up once more by some 200–250 pesos a year.

In order to show how the households used their income, tables 15 and 16 give the most important expenditures—for living and occupational activities respectively. Table 15

TABLE 15

Principal Annual Living Expenditures of Households
Sampled in Mitla, 1963

(In Current Pesos)

HOUSE-HOLD NUMBER	FOOD	CLOTH-ING	UTILI-TIES	OTHER	TOTAL
1	4,160	800	360[a]	150[b]	5,570
2	3,100	600	90[c]	700[d]	4,490
3	12,050	2,100	240[e]	915[f]	15,305
4	undet.	undet.	undet.	undet.	5,000[g]
5	5,475	600	1,680[a]	1,000[h]	8,755
6	3,470	450	325[a]	. . . .	4,245
7	3,830	500	80[c]	. . . .	4,410
8	3,650	600	95[c]	1,500[i]	5,845

[a] Cost of electricity and water service.
[b] Purchase price of two piglets.
[c] Electric bill.
[d] Medical expenditures.
[e] Water bill.
[f] Medical and school expenditures.
[g] Estimate. (Expenditures incurred on all items by this household, but amounts not determined.)
[h] Difference between the value of gifts received (1,000 pesos) and the value of gifts given (2,000 pesos).
[i] Cost of funeral.

shows that food constituted the largest single expenditure; from 30 to 60 percent of this was accounted for by the cost of three or four kilograms of corn. Most households also consumed vegetables and root crops which were sometimes grown in the fields; their value, however, was not obtained and consequently both the value of "other agricultural products" (third column of table 14) and the food expenditures (second column of table 15) are somewhat understated. Moreover, the food expenditures correspond to normal every-day consumption and do not include the cost of the special food consumed during family celebrations, holidays, and other festive occasions.

Expenditures on clothing were considerably smaller than food expenditures. The variations shown by the table reflect the fact that there were peasants who wore only rustic cloth-ing and either went barefoot or wore sandals while there were others who wore shoes and more modern, expensive gar-ments. All the households incurred expenditures on water service, on electricity, or on both. The large utility expen-diture of household 5 is explained by the several real estate properties owned by the head of the household.

In the opinion of some of the townspeople, certain tradi-tional feasts were beginning to lose their importance; how-ever, there were still occasions when large expenditures could not be avoided. Household 8, as shown by the fifth column of the table, had to incur a heavy expense for a funeral. And it should be noted that this household was considered poor. A man of means would have had to purchase for a funeral, among other things, one steer, one pig, twelve turkeys, 400 kilograms of corn, several kilograms of kidneys, three bags of flour, and thirty cartons of beer; in addition he also would have had to pay for the services of a baker. To meet these eventualities a household had its savings as first recourse, but if these were not enough, the incurrence of a debt was customary.

To conclude the explanation of table 15, it may be added that most of the "other" expenditures shown by the fifth column of the table represent the cost of emergencies which all the households occasionally faced. It is interesting to note that in contrast to the variations found in income, the total living expenditures shown by the last column have much more uniformity.

The expenditures incurred in farming and in other occupational activities are examined in table 16. Not all the

TABLE 16

Principal Annual Occupational Expenditures of
Households Sampled in Mitla, 1963

(In Current Pesos)

HOUSE-HOLD NUM-BER	HIRE OF LABOR AND EQUIP-MENT	SEED AND ANIMAL FEED	CAPITAL AND OTHER	TOTAL OCCUPA-TIONAL EXPENDI-TURES	TOTAL LIVING AND OCCUPA-TIONAL EXPENDI-TURES[a]	AVAIL-ABLE FOR OTHER EXPENDI-TURES AND SAVINGS[b]
1	200[c]	540	90[d] 150[e]	980	6,550	7,200
2	80[f] 160[e]	710	25[d]	975	5,465	−1,045
3	....	....	150[d]	150	15,455	6,145
4	undet.	undet.	undet.	2,300[g]	7,300	1,860
5	3,960[f] 600[e]	1,310	150[d] 2,200[h]	8,220	16,975	5,310
6	....	1,330	70[d]	1,400	5,645	−1,720
7	100[e]	590	15[d]	705	5,115	−825
8	....	990	30[d]	1,020	6,865	−1,305

[a] Total occupational expenditures of fifth column plus last column of table 15.
[b] Total living and occupational expenditures deducted from total earned income (seventh column) of table 14.
[c] Hire of oxen.
[d] Taxes.
[e] Cost of transport of crops.
[f] Hire of labor.
[g] Estimate.
[h] Cost of water pump.

quantities shown on this table are out-of-pocket expenditures; the animal feed and the seed, for instance, came almost exclusively from the household's production of corn, corn stalks, and husks. However, since the value of these items was not deducted from the value of the output, they are shown as actual expenditures. The hire of oxen shown in the second column is another item that may not represent an actual expenditure. There were times when farmers who had an excess of corn stalks and husks bartered them in exchange for plowing services.

With the exception of animal feed the other occupational expenditures were relatively small; especially the expenditures on seed since the amount needed did not usually exceed sixteen kilograms per hectare. Only one expenditure—the purchase of a water pump by the head of household 5, which was used to irrigate the crops in his backyard—can be regarded as investment, although the expenditures on animal feed can be considered maintenance of capital. In general, compared to the living expenditures, the occupational expenditures were much smaller. Depreciation of capital equipment was not included in the latter, but it was probably small.

The last column of table 16 shows that no household belonging to the low economic category had any money left for other expenditures or for savings. Actually, the presence of these deficits is partly due to unusual circumstances. To begin with, 1963 was not a good agricultural year since the corn output was low and since almost the entire production of beans was lost. The head of household 2 said that he normally had savings of 150 pesos per year but that in 1963 he had had large medical expenditures, and this is why he had a deficit. The deficit of household 8 is explained by the funeral costs incurred by the family, and that of household 7 by its almost nil corn crop. The head of household 6 stated that he was unable to save and that when emergencies arose he had to borrow money. Since he did not indicate that 1963 had been a particularly bad year, he may have understated his income; and therefore his deficit, if any, may be overstated. In spite of the bad year and the deficits recorded, none of the households had to borrow money in 1963 to meet any of its expenditures. The households in the medium and high economic categories, moreover, had ample balances left for other expenditures and savings, as the last column of table 16 shows.

For Mitla this completes the household survey data and the presentation of the empirical material. The task of analysis remains, but the next item is to report the household survey data for the other villages. The next village in the survey is Chan Kom, and first to be examined are some general characteristics of the households sampled.

Table 17 shows that in Chan Kom all the household heads,

TABLE 17

General Characteristics of Households Sampled
in Chan Kom, 1963

HOUSE-HOLD NUMBER	NUMBER OF PERSONS	NUMBER OF EARNERS	MAIN AND SECONDARY OCCUPATION OF HEAD	HIGHEST SCHOOL GRADE OF HEAD	AGE OF HEAD	ECONOMIC LEVEL OF HOUSE-HOLD[a]
1	7	1	Farmer, hunter	3	36	M
2	9	2	Farmer, mason	8	31	M
3	9	2	Farmer, merchant	undet.	45	H
4	9	2	Farmer	1	45	L
5	4	1	Farmer	3	30	L
6	2	1	Merchant, miller	2	60	H
7	2	1	Farmer	0	60	M
8	8	1	Farmer	undet.	30	M
9	10	2	Farmer, merchant	5	40	L
10	5	2	Farmer	0	58	L

[a] High, medium, or low. Level based on the general regard in which the household was held and on assets and income.

with the exception of one (6), had farming as their main occupation. All of them engaged in the sale of corn, eggs, and cattle, but only those that owned a business (such as a store) are shown as merchants. In no case did a household head have a father who was not a farmer. Contrary to what was found in Mitla, where practically all those interviewed were natives, in Chan Kom several of the households sampled had immigrated in recent times. Households 4, 9, and 10 had been residing in the village for two years; the head of household 6 had been a resident for ten years; and the head of household 7 had arrived when he was ten years old. On the basis of the sample the households had 6.5 members on the average.

The classifications of the last column were arrived at following a procedure similar to that employed for Mitla. In Chan Kom, however, while differences in wealth and income were present, the majority of the people belonged to the medium economic category. Not only did they dress alike, eat the same food, and live in more or less similar houses, but because they had equal rights to the use of land, differences in income and wealth were minimized. Nevertheless, there were some persons who lived in masonry houses, who had water wells in their backyards, and who owned a larger number of cattle; so economic categories still existed. As in the case of Mitla, however, there were no families which were "very poor" in relation to the others. Regarding the educational level of the household heads, it can be seen that with the exception of the head of household 2 (who acted as clerk of the civil registry office) their schooling tended to be rather low.

The most important assets owned by the Chan Kom households are given by table 18. First, as the table shows, all ten households owned their houses. Not all of these were made of masonry, but six had water wells (see notes to table 18). Since the bush freely provided most of the construction materials, wattle-walled houses were not expensive to construct. The head of household 9, for instance, spent only 850 pesos to build his house—350 pesos for the lot and 500 pesos for materials and labor. A more modern house (with tiled roof and floors, windows, water well in the backyard, etc.) was of course much more expensive to construct—as the value of the house of household 8 illustrates. The ejido system, in combination with the abundant supply of land, allowed every man to cultivate as much land as he wished; and in some instances rather large tracts were cultivated. However, the second column of the table shows that most plots comprised from four to eight hectares.

TABLE 18

Principal Assets Owned by Households

Sampled in Chan Kom, 1963

(Current Market Value in Pesos)

HOUSEHOLD NUMBER	HOUSE	LAND[a]	ANIMALS[b]	TOOLS	PRODUCTION GOODS	DURABLES[c]	JEWELRY	TOTAL VALUE[d]
1	1,950[e]	16	1,020	75	600[f]	75	1,800	5,520
2	8,200[g]	8	810	undet.	1,800[h]	800	undet.	11,610
3	4,700[i]	8	1,020	undet.	28,000[h] undet.[j]	800	3,000	37,520
4	750[k]	12	300	125	1,300[h] 300[f]	....	700	3,475
5	2,400[e]	4	765	100	....	....	600	3,865
6	5,700[i]	..	1,200	undet.	7,000[i] undet.[m]	800	undet.	14,700
7	3,500[n]	8	750	undet.	14,000[h]	....	950	19,200
8	13,500[i]	13	540	undet.	4,200[h] 300[f]	1,000	undet.	19,450
9	2,050[e]	4	800	125	1,800[h] 600[f]	....	undet.	4,375
10	750[k]	8	650	125	3,200[h] 300[f]	900	1,300	7,225

[a] Hectares of land cultivated—mainly ejido.
[b] Figures include the average village price of chickens (15 pesos), turkeys (60 pesos), and hogs (500 pesos).
[c] Figures include average village price of rifles (75 pesos) and sewing machines (800-1,000 pesos).
[d] Excludes value of land.
[e] House with masonry walls, thatched roof, and water well.
[f] Value of horses—on the basis of an average price of 300 pesos.
[g] Two masonry houses with water wells.
[h] Value of cattle—on the basis of an average price of 450-850 pesos per head.
[i] Masonry house with water well.
[j] This household also owned homemade irrigation equipment, some beehives, and a grocery store, but their value was not determined.
[k] House with wattle or masonry walls and thatched roof.
[l] Value of corn mills.
[m] Ownership of a grocery store (value undetermined).
[n] Masonry house without water well.

Ownership of animals was common, particularly of hogs, cattle, chickens, and horses. At times epizootics appeared with severe consequences. In 1963 an epizootic of hogs appeared which caused serious losses not only of hogs but of other animals as well.[2] When animals became infected the people tried various cures, but for the most part these were not effective and epizootics simply ran their course. Once an epizootic struck it was impossible to sell the animals whether they had become infected or not; sick animals were of course unsalable, and when the news of an epizootic spread there were no buyers willing to take even the healthy ones, since there was no guarantee of their remaining healthy.

In spite of the periodic recurrence of epizootics, the number of cattle had continued to grow. Furthermore, the native breed was being displaced by more valuable breeds, especially by the variety known as Cebu which seemed to thrive in Chan Kom and in other parts of Mexico. As the column on "production goods" shows, seven households owned cattle and five households owned horses. Two households (3 and 6) owned grocery stores, and one of them (6) also owned two corn mills. The value of the stores, unfortunately, could not be obtained.

Many families also owned durables, which in Chan Kom consisted mainly of sewing machines. All the families sampled also owned jewelry. Some of this jewelry was acquired by the women at the time of their marriage, but most men also made purchases of gold chains, rings, bracelets, and earrings for both their wives and teen-age daughters. Asked to state the reason why he owned jewelry, the head of household 3 said that people borrowed money from him, leaving the jewelry as security, and that in many cases it was forfeited. The head of household 1 stated that jewelry had the advantage of being easy to pawn in case of need. The head of household 7 was the only one who was against owning jewelry on the grounds that when the need arose it was usually sold at a loss.

2. Households 1, 3, 4, and 5 lost five hogs each; household 3 lost four head of cattle (two of which were slaughtered before becoming infected); households 2 and 9 lost two hogs each; household 7 lost three cows and three calves; and household 10 lost two calves. This means that eight families out of ten suffered losses, the total loss amounting to some 11,430 pesos.

Information about the income of the Chan Kom households is presented in table 19. In most cases the corn crop

TABLE 19

Annual Income, by Principal Sources, of Households
Sampled in Chan Kom, 1963

(In Current Pesos)

HOUSE-HOLD NUM-BER	CORN OUT-PUT[a]	OTHER AGRICUL-TURAL PROD-UCTS[b]	ANIMAL PROD-UCTS[c]	ARTS AND CRAFTS	OTHER SOURCES	TOTAL EARNED INCOME	PER CAPITA INCOME
1	6,240	640	7,720[d]	200[e]	550[f]	15,350	2,230
2	2,680	325	1,280	1,220[g]	1,440[h]	6,945	790
3	7,140	240	2,625	600[e]	2,400[i]	25,605[j]	2,845
					2,200[k]		
					10,400[l]		
4	3,210	325	1,280	....	600[l]	5,415	601
5	1,785	1,000	1,970[m]	....	....	4,755	1,188
6	....	....	3,080	....	900[f]	21,660	10,830
					17,680[n]		
7	3,570	760	2,955	....	5,000[k]	12,285	6,142
8	5,000	690	1,460	undet.	1,800[k]	8,950	1,118
9	1,785	75	1,020	....	600[f]	3,880	388
					400[k]		
10	1,070	undet.	1,020	400[e]	undet.[l]	3,340	668
					850[k]		

[a] Based on an average price of 0.85 pesos per kg. of corn.
[b] Includes the market value of vegetables, root crops, and fruits.
[c] Figures include the value of the production of eggs (0.35 pesos each), the value of venison (10 pesos per kg.), and the value of chickens (average price 15 pesos) and turkeys (average price 60 pesos) sold.
[d] Includes 2,320 pesos from sale of eggs, 4,800 pesos from sale of venison, and 600 pesos from sale of chickens.
[e] Income from sewing and embroidering.
[f] Income from sale of hogs.
[g] Includes 500 pesos from wages as mason and 720 pesos from sewing.
[h] Represents salary earned in civil registry office.
[i] Wages.
[j] This figure does not include the proceeds from the sale of eighteen containers of honey.
[k] Income from sale of cattle.
[l] Income from commerce.
[m] Includes 1,370 pesos from sale of eggs and 600 pesos from sale of venison.
[n] Income from commerce and milling.

constituted the main source of income, although substantial earnings were also obtained from the sale of poultry, eggs, and livestock. Surplus corn and eggs were usually sold to the local stores which in turn made weekly shipments by truck to Mérida and Valladolid. At other times some men took their goods directly to the city markets. Income from the sale of cattle was not uncommon, but unless intended to meet an emergency it was usually kept as circulating capital, that is, ready to be reinvested on livestock. Income from arts and crafts was small, but commerce made a sizeable contribution to the income of the two households (3 and 6) that operated grocery stores. As a rule farmers of Chan Kom produced corn in excess of their needs. In 1963 only one household (10) had a crop so poor that it was inadequate to satisfy the household's needs. Finally, sewing machines had been gaining popularity, and most families that owned one were putting it to good use making clothes for others. In this manner they were able to earn some extra income each year.

If the total amount of corn produced (approximately 38,220 kg.) is divided by the number of hectares of land on which it was grown (81.0 ha.), it can be found that 471 kilograms of corn were obtained per hectare; a yield which confirmed the decline in the productivity of the land.

All the household heads interviewed stated that their situation was better in 1963 than in past years and that they foresaw a continuance of their progress. The varying size of the households (see second column of table 17) accounts for much of the variation in the per capita income figures shown by the last column of table 19, although considerable variation can also be observed in total earned income. It is to be noted that the households with the highest total income (1, 3, 6, and 7) obtained the largest part of it from sources other than the output of corn. The head of household 1 was a deer hunter, and his income from the sale of venison was almost as large as his income from corn. Customarily he kept about one-half of the venison for family consumption, and he sold the other half in the city of Valladolid. In the table only the half actually sold is included under the "animal products" column. In the case of households 3, 6, and 7, commerce and the sale of cattle were the main non-corn sources of income. The average per capita income of the households sampled was 1,662 pesos, a figure somewhat lower than that found in Mitla but easily explained by Chan Kom's larger average household.[3]

Next to be examined are the main living expenditures incurred by the households in 1963. Table 20 shows that in

TABLE 20

Principal Annual Living Expenditures of Households
Sampled in Chan Kom, 1963

(In Current Pesos)

HOUSE-HOLD NUMBER	FOOD	CLOTHING	OTHER	TOTAL
1	3,100	300	250[a]	3,650
2	4,000	200	250[a]	4,450
3	5,475	300	4,350[b]	10,125
4	3,650	600	. . . .	4,250
5	3,300	300	. . . .	3,600
6	2,550	200	. . . .	2,750
7	2,600	200	200[c]	3,000
8	4,380	600	1,160[d]	6,140
9	3,300	300	500[e]	4,100
10	3,100	400	900[e]	4,400

[a] Purchase of jewelry.
[b] Includes purchase of jewelry (150 pesos), medical expenditures (200 pesos), and cost of a wedding (4,000 pesos).
[c] Medical expenditures.
[d] Includes purchase of a sewing machine (1,000 pesos) and cost of a family celebration (160 pesos).
[e] Purchase of a sewing machine.

Chan Kom—as in Mitla—food was by far the largest item of expenditure, followed by expenditures on clothing and

3. This consisted of 6.5 persons in contrast to Mitla's 5.5.

jewelry. The figures shown by the food column are probably
more reliable than those shown by the clothing column. The
reason is that since corn accounted for such a large portion
of the diet—the other portion consisting of eggs, beans, meat,
coffee, chocolate, various vegetables, root crops, and fruits—
it was not too difficult to obtain reasonable estimates of the
weekly food bill. Accurate clothing expenditures, however,
were difficult to get because nobody bothered to keep track
of them. Most of the persons interviewed would show sur-
prise at being asked for this information, and there seemed
to be a tendency—both in Chan Kom and in the other villages—to understate the actual amount spent. There was little
diversity in clothing which may explain in part the uniformity
shown by the clothing expenditures. Such uniformity, however, does not seem justified for some households when their
size is taken into account, and so for some of them these expenditures may contain a large margin of error. Of the average—as will be explained at the end of the chapter—these
clothing expenditures are reasonable.

As indicated previously, in Chan Kom it was fashionable
to own jewelry, and most families bought it at various times.
Out of the ten households sampled, three had spent money
on jewelry during 1963. Household 3, one of the important
households of Chan Kom, had a wedding which, as table 20
shows, occasioned a sizeable expenditure. Lastly, the table
lists purchases of sewing machines by households 8 and 10.

The principal occupational expenditures are given in
table 21. The second column shows that some households
had expenditures on the hire of labor and horses. The practice of hiring labor was sometimes difficult to avoid because
the agricultural system was based on the cultivation of relatively large tracts. In addition some households had only one
adult male, which further necessitated the use of hired labor.

The hire of horses was necessary for those who lacked the
means to transport the crops to the home. The expenditures
for this purpose were relatively small and usually spread
over a period of time. Most farmers left the corn ears on the

TABLE 21

Principal Annual Occupational Expenditures of
Households Sampled in Chan Kom, 1963

(In Current Pesos)

HOUSE-HOLD NUMBER	HIRE OF LABOR AND EQUIPMENT	SEED AND ANIMAL FEED	CAPITAL AND OTHER	TOTAL OCCUPATIONAL EXPENDITURES	TOTAL LIVING AND OCCUPATIONAL EXPENDITURES[a]	AVAILABLE FOR OTHER EXPENDITURES AND SAVINGS[b]
1	900[c]	1,390	240[d]	2,530	6,180	9,170
2	300[c] 150[e]	1,000	....	1,450	5,900	1,045
3	....	1,315	885[d] 60[f] 180[g]	2,440	12,565	13,040
4	....	720	....	720	4,970	445
5	....	810	100[d]	910	4,510	245
6	....	550	400[d] 75[f]	1,025	3,775	17,885
7	350[c] 50[e]	695	....	1,095	4,095	8,190
8	1,650[c]	665	1,500[h]	3,815	9,955	−1,005
9	....	655	50[d] 50[g] 2,050[i]	2,805	6,905	−3,025
10	....	625	....	625	5,025	−1,685

[a] Total occupational expenditures of fifth column plus last column of table 20.
[b] Total living and occupational expenditures deducted from total earned income (seventh column) of table 19.
[c] Hire of labor.
[d] Transportation and travel expenditures.
[e] Hire of horses.
[f] Taxes.
[g] Purchase of trees.
[h] Cost of water well.
[i] Construction cost of house and water well.

plant itself or stored part of the corn crop in granaries built on the fields. This meant that the corn was not transported to the homes until it was needed, either for sale or for family consumption, and most of the time this took place gradually.

The expenditures on corn seed were rather small; those

on animal feed were considerably larger and were accounted for by the value of the corn fed to chickens, pigs, and to horses when they were being used to transport the crops. Cattle were kept on the fields where they ate corn stalks, corn husks, and vegetation found in the bush. For this reason, the cost of their maintenance does not appear on the table.[4] When not used for the transport of crops, horses were also kept on the fields.

The "capital and other" expenditures appearing in the fourth column of table 21 represent purchases of trees, construction costs of houses and water wells, transportation charges, cost of traveling to the city markets, and taxes. The latter were paid by the store owners and consisted of mercantile taxes levied by the state government. All the stores in Chan Kom paid them, and curiously enough they were the only payments unmistakenly acknowledged as taxes. Of course, as explained in chapter 3, the amounts effectively contributed to the government were much larger, but the people did not think of other payments or contributions as taxes. The last column shows that two store owners had large sums available for "other expenditures and savings." One of them (from household 3) expressed his intention to buy a truck upon completion of the improvements to the road, and the other (head of 6) said that he was accumulating his savings to start a cattle ranch.

In 1964 the head of household 1 was building a new masonry house. He also intended to build an oven and hire a baker for one year to teach his sons how to bake bread. The head of household 4, in spite of his poor corn crop in 1963, said that in 1964 he was going to use his savings to purchase two head of cattle.

The construction of water wells and of a house caused the deficits of households 8 and 9 respectively. The latter also

4. Contrary to what happened in Mitla, in Chan Kom corn stalks and husks had no commercial value, which is why they were not incorporated in the "other agricultural products" column of table 19.

had a large medical expenditure which forced the family to borrow 300 pesos on which interest of 5 percent a month was being paid. Except for this sum, the head of household 9 was free of debt, and in March 1964 he was able to invest 200 pesos in the opening of a place where he sold refreshments.[5] The head of household 10 was the only one who made clear that his poor corn crop had meant a particularly bad year. He stated that it had been unnecessary to borrow money but that since there were a few months to go before the next harvest he was not ruling out the possibility of a loan. The size of his deficit, however, was actually smaller than that shown because the two earners in the household, besides farming, also worked as laborers but were unable to state how much they had earned, and thus their wages were not included in the household's income. No household found it necessary to borrow money in 1963.

Soteapan is the next village in the survey, but before the data are presented a word of explanation is in order. It was mentioned in chapter 4 that until 1960 Soteapan had not been affected by the agrarian reform but that in that year new allocations of land had been started. This had created an abnormal situation because many farmers had abandoned lands which they traditionally had cultivated, while others were farming reduced pieces of land uncertain about whether they would be allowed to keep them or whether they would lose them to some other community. At the time of the author's visit to the village, the situation was still very much unsettled, and it became difficult to find households that had not been affected. For this reason only three households were interviewed: two of them because they were studied by Foster and hence afforded excellent cases for making comparisons, and the third because it seemed to typify Soteapan's average

---

5. This man told the author that he decided to start his business after making a trip to Mérida where he saw how refreshments were prepared.

household in 1963, that is, one that had been badly disrupted by the changing conditions.

Table 22 presents the general characteristics of the house-

TABLE 22

General Characteristics of Households Sampled
in Soteapan, 1963

HOUSE-HOLD NUMBER	NUMBER OF PERSONS	NUMBER OF EARNERS	MAIN AND SECONDARY OCCUPATION OF HEAD	HIGHEST SCHOOL GRADE OF HEAD	AGE OF HEAD	ECONOMIC LEVEL OF HOUSE-HOLD[a]
1	6	1	Farmer	1	58	M
2	9	3	Farmer	0	53	M
3	10	3	Farmer	0	56	M

[a] High, medium, or low. Level based on the general regard in which the household was held and on assets and income.

holds. The data show that the households, with an average size of more than eight persons, tended to be rather large. All three had earners who made a living solely from agriculture, and all of them included members who were natives. The heads of the households had two characteristics in common; first, their fathers had also been farmers, and second, they had practically no schooling. Households 1 and 2 were the ones studied by Foster, household 3 being the one picked out by the author to round out the sample.

The principal assets owned by the households are presented in table 23. Ownership of houses seemed to be the rule in Soteapan, and it applied to the three households sampled. For some reason unknown to the author, there were practically no well-constructed masonry houses; most of them were made of wattle or sheet metal and thatch. Most households owned a few animals (including beasts of burden), and even though the agricultural system was mainly of the digging stick type, three or four households owned teams of oxen which they used for plowing their own lands—or those of others, for a fee. In 1963 an epizootic swept through the

TABLE 23

Principal Assets Owned by Households

Sampled in Soteapan, 1963

(Current Market Value in Pesos)

HOUSE-HOLD NUMBER	HOUSE	LAND[a]	ANI-MALS[b]	TOOLS	PRODUC-TION GOODS	DURA-BLES	OTHER[c]	TOTAL VALUE[d]
1	1,700[e]	3	150	50	1,500[f]	1,200[g]	1,500	4,600
2	700	3	975	400	400[h]	....	200	2,475
3	700	5	...	1,150	4,680[i]	....	....	6,530

[a] Hectares of land cultivated—mainly ejido.
[b] Figures include the average village price of chickens (15 pesos), and hogs (300 pesos).
[c] Shown is the number of coffee trees, not their value.
[d] Excludes value of land and value of coffee trees.
[e] Represents ownership of two houses.
[f] Value of mules—on the basis of an average price of 750 pesos.
[g] Value of a sewing machine.
[h] Value of a horse.
[i] Of this sum 2,210 pesos represents the value of mules, 2,250 pesos represent the value of oxen, and 220 pesos represent the value of a burro.

village and many households suffered severe losses, including the three households sampled.[6]

Coffee trees were another item of wealth that was common to many households. The head of household 3 had a coffee plantation of some 1,000 trees. It was situated at a distance of twelve kilometers from the village, and since it was difficult to obtain laborers to work in it, when the land was awarded as ejido to another village, he abandoned it. One of the five hectares of land that he was actually cultivating was planted with about 6,000 pineapple plants, but it seemed that this land had also been awarded to another village, and thus he wondered whether he would have to surrender it. His other four hectares were the only ones that he thought he would be able to keep. On them he grew corn and beans, and since

6. The losses suffered by the households (and their value in pesos) were the following: household 1, two large pigs (750) and twelve chickens (180); household 2, five pigs (500) and ten chickens (80); and household 3, five pigs (1,500) and fifteen chickens (210).

he had cultivated them continuously for a number of years, he had staked a claim by erecting a barb wire fence around them.

The head of household 2 also owned coffee trees and also suffered some losses. In his case the loss amounted to 300 trees. As table 23 shows, he still owned 200 of them, but it was not certain whether he was going to keep these either, because they were planted on a piece of land that seemed to be in the way of the road under construction. Of the three households, the first was the only one that had not yet been affected by the redistribution of land.

Shown in table 24 is the income earned by the households

TABLE 24

Annual Income, by Principal Sources, of Households

Sampled in Soteapan, 1963

(In Current Pesos)

HOUSE- HOLD NUM- BER	CORN OUT- PUT[a]	OTHER AGRICUL- TURAL PROD- UCTS[b]	ANI- MAL PROD- UCTS	ARTS AND CRAFTS	OTHER SOURCES	TOTAL EARNED INCOME	PER CAPITA INCOME
1	2,140	4,795[c]	1,300[d]	. . .	3,200[e]	11,435	1,905
2	2,425	600	. . . .	500[f]	. . . .	3,525	391
3	1,700	3,100[g]	. . . .	. . .	280[h]	5,080	508

[a] Based on an average price of 0.85 pesos per kg. of corn.
[b] Includes the value of the following items: coffee crop (based on an average price of 4.75 pesos per kg. of coffee), bean crop (1.70 pesos per kg.), rice crop (1.00 pesos per kg., unshelled), and the output of various fruits.
[c] Includes 2,375 pesos from sale of coffee, 1,740 pesos from sale of various fruits, and 680 pesos from sale of beans.
[d] Income from sale of eggs—based on an average price of 0.50 pesos each.
[e] Income from sale of cattle.
[f] Income from manufacture of cots.
[g] Includes 750 pesos from sale of rice, 1,500 pesos from sale of pineapples, and 850 pesos from sale of beans.
[h] Income from rent of oxen and mules.

in 1963. The income of household 1 was about average, and except for the sale of cattle the income from the other sources could be considered normal. Households 2 and 3, on the other hand, had below-normal income, caused mainly by the loss of earnings from coffee. The last column of the table shows that the per capita income of these two households was quite low; something which is explained by the combination of low earnings and large families (9 and 10 members respectively).

The head of household 1 was the only one who felt that his condition had improved in the last few years and that his prospects appeared promising. The other two felt that in past years they had of course been better off and that their prospects were quite problematic. To illustrate his past prosperity, the head of household 3 stated that in 1956 he was able to enter into a contract for the purchase of a truck. After he had paid 6,000 pesos, he fell behind on his payments and lost it. Partly as a result of this incident he believed that since 1956 his situation had deteriorated.

The head of household 2 indicated that in addition to the problems caused by the changing conditions, 1963 had been a bad year. The coffee trees that he still had were old and did not produce as much as in previous years. Then, it seemed that the productivity of his land had gone down, and therefore his corn crops had been getting smaller every year. In 1963 he had to borrow 200 pesos to meet his expenditures, and for a few months he had to pay monthly interest of 2.5 percent on the loan. One of his sons manufactured cots at home and this provided additional income. He thought that the manufacture of cots could be increased, but the authorities in the surrounding villages did not permit their sale and consequently only a few were made.

It is interesting to note that when the cultivation of corn was accompanied by the cultivation of other crops, the income derived from the latter could be greater than the income derived from the former. This, at any rate, is what happened in the case of households 1 and 3, both of which had a larger income from agricultural products other than corn, than from corn itself.

The principal living expenditures of the households are

TABLE 25

Principal Annual Living Expenditures of Households

Sampled in Soteapan, 1963

(In Current Pesos)

HOUSE-HOLD NUMBER	FOOD	CLOTHING	OTHER	TOTAL
1	2,920	200	200[a] 85[b]	3,405
2	4,200	500	200[a]	4,900
3	3,850	1,000	. . .	4,850

[a] Medical expenditures.
[b] Cost of electricity.

shown by table 25. In Soteapan, as in the other two villages examined thus far, food accounted for the largest single expenditure. The food column in table 25 includes the value of the corn, eggs, and poultry consumed directly on the farm plus the value of some purchases made to supplement the basic staples. The total cost of the food actually consumed, however, was somewhat greater than the amounts shown because the diet was also supplemented by numerous vegetables, root crops, and fish, but their value was not included in the table. The other living expenditures were relatively small. The clothing expenditures, given the large size of the households, seem to have been underestimated, particularly those of households 1 and 2.

The examination of the principal occupational expenditures concludes the household survey of Soteapan. The expenditures of the households shown by table 26 are self-explanatory, but the figures of the last column require some explanation. The large surplus of household 1 was due in part to the sale of livestock in the amount of 3,200 pesos. Even without this sale, however, a rather large sum would still have been available either to meet other expenditures or for savings. The head of the household, in fact, confirmed this by explaining that he was able to save every year. Since

TABLE 26

Principal Annual Occupational Expenditures of
Households Sampled in Soteapan, 1963
(In Current Pesos)

HOUSE-HOLD NUMBER	SEED AND ANIMAL FEED	CAPITAL AND OTHER	TOTAL OCCUPA-TIONAL EXPENDI-TURES	TOTAL LIVING AND OCCUPA-TIONAL EXPENDI-TURES[a]	AVAILABLE FOR OTHER EXPENDI-TURES AND SAVINGS[b]
1	545	undet.	545	3,950	7,485
2	1,010	50[c]	1,160	6,060	–2,535
		100[d]			
3	720	undet.	720	5,570	–490

[a] Total occupational expenditures of fourth column plus last column of table 25.
[b] Total living and occupational expenditures deducted from total earned income (seventh column) of table 24.
[c] Taxes.
[d] Purchase of tools.

he had not sustained any loss of land, this seemed entirely plausible.

In contrast to the good showing of household 1, the other two households registered deficits. In spite of this the head of household 3 said he had had no need to borrow money in 1963. The head of household 2, as already indicated, had to borrow 200 pesos, but by the spring of 1964 the loan had been repaid and the family was free of debt. The expenditures shown for this family do not appear unreasonable, but the income may have been understated—especially in view of the fact that there were three earners in the household—and consequently the size of the deficit may be unduly large. The head of the household, though, claimed that his earnings had been declining. The main reason he gave for this was a drop in the corn yield. He explained that whereas some years ago from 1.6 hectares of land he was able to get more than 2,000 kilograms of corn, in the past few years, from 3 hectares, he could not even get 3,000 kilograms.

TABLE 27

General Characteristics of Households

Sampled in Tepoztlán, 1963

HOUSE-HOLD NUMBER	NUMBER OF PERSONS	NUMBER OF EARNERS	MAIN AND SECONDARY OCCUPATION OF HEAD	HIGHEST SCHOOL GRADE OF HEAD	AGE OF HEAD	ECONOMIC LEVEL OF HOUSE-HOLD[a]
1	7	1	Farmer	6	36	M
2	7	1	Laborer	2	35	L
3	10	1	Mason	4	40	L
4	8	2	Farmer	3	57	M
5	8	1	Farmer	2	37	L
6	3	1	Shoemaker	8	55	M
7	6	1	Farmer	0	86	M
8	4	1	Laborer	3	37	L
9	6	1	Mason, farmer	4	43	M
10	4	1	Mason, carpenter	6	39	M
11	8	3	Farmer	3	68	M
12	2	1	Farmer	3	49	L
13	10	2	Farmer, mason	2	44	M
14	5	3	Butcher	0	69	M
15	3	1	Farmer	1	85	M

[a] High, medium, or low. Level based on the general regard in which the household was held and on assets and income.

Turning to the last of the villages surveyed, table 27 gives the general characteristics of the households sampled. The data show that in Tepoztlán there was considerable variation in occupations, although farmers still constituted the majority. Those mainly engaged in farming had fathers who had also been farmers, while those engaged in trades were sons of tradesmen. Thus the father of the head of household 6 was a shoemaker, the fathers of the heads of households 9 and 10 were masons, and the father of the head of household 14 was a butcher. Most of the households had only one earner, and all the heads were natives of the village. As a rule large households with only one earner had several small children or else they had old people, particularly old women. With the exception of the heads of households 7 and 14 (both of them rather old men), all the others had had some schooling. Four of them (2, 3, 5, and 9) worked at various times as farm laborers in the United States, and the head of household 7 had a grandson who had done similar work. None of the households was considered wealthy; as the last column of the table shows they all belonged either to the medium or to the low economic category. On the basis of the sample, the average household consisted of six persons.

Table 28 lists the principal assets owned by the households. The second column shows that with the exception of households 3 and 8 all the others owned the houses in which they lived. These houses were made of masonry or adobes, and they usually included a backyard with fruit trees. In spite of the fact that the real estate market in Tepoztlán had been an active one, opinions seemed to vary concerning the value of real estate, and therefore perhaps it ought to be repeated that the house values shown are rough estimates. The head of household 2, however, seemed to have a good idea of the cost of his house, because he had built it with the savings accumulated in three seasons of farm work in the United States.

Six households did not own land. In three cases (households 3, 10, and 14) it did not matter, because the household heads did not engage in farming. In the other three cases it did matter; to be without land meant that the head of household 5 had to farm on rented land, and the heads of households 2 and 8 had to become wage laborers. It should be added that there was a third possibility open to landless farmers: they could enter into a sharecropping agreement.

Ownership of animals was extensive, and many families owned at least a few chickens and turkeys. Tractors and trucks were acquiring importance as items of wealth, but the ownership of oxen and pack animals was still prevalent. Some farmers were using a combination of tractor and oxen to plow their fields. One household (15) owned a dairy which included twenty-five head of cattle. Many families owned

TABLE 28
Principal Assets Owned by Households
Sampled in Tepoztlán, 1963
(Current Market Value in Pesos)

HOUSE-HOLD NUMBER	HOUSE	LAND[a]	ANIMALS[b]	TOOLS	PRODUCTION GOODS	DURABLES[c]	OTHER	TOTAL VALUE[d]
1	20,000	2.50[e]	750	300	4,800[f] 2,000[g] 1,500[h]	300	....	29,350
2	12,000	....	225	undet.	1,000[g]	300	....	13,525
3	....	....	undet.	undet.	undet.	300	....	300
4	18,000	7.00[i]	775	undet.	3,500[f] 7,200[h] 14,400[j]	900	....	43,875
5	11,000	....	125	undet.	....	1,200	....	12,325
6	13,000	3.00[i]	...	1,000	2,300[h]	1,000	....	17,300
7	19,000	4.00[e] 1.00[i]	250	undet.	3,000[f] 900[j]	2,000	....	25,150
8	....	....	...	150	....	....	....	150
9	15,000	undet.	125	undet.	....	900	undet.[k]	16,025
10	14,000	....	220	undet.	....	....	....	14,220
11	16,000	2.00[i]	1,400	undet.	6,000[f] 3,000[g]	undet.	....	26,400
12	11,000	1.00[i]	150	undet.	....	....	....	11,150
13	22,000	3.00[i]	700	undet.	900[j]	300	undet.[k]	23,600
14	14,000	....	400	undet.	....	300	....	14,700
15	18,000	undet.	75	undet.	1,000[g] 25,000[h] 900[j]	undet.	....	44,975

[a] Hectares of land cultivated.
[b] Figures include the average village price of chickens (25 pesos), turkeys (75 pesos), and hogs (700 pesos).
[c] Figures include the average village price of radios (300 pesos), sewing machines (900 pesos), and gas stoves (800 pesos).
[d] Excludes value of land.
[e] Size of ejido holdings.
[f] Value of oxen—on the basis of a price of 3,000-4,800 pesos per team.
[g] Value of mules—on the basis of an average price of 1,000 pesos.
[h] Value of cattle—on the basis of a price of 575-1,500 pesos per head.
[i] Size of private land holdings.
[j] Value of horses—on the basis of an average price of 900 pesos.
[k] Savings account.

radios and sewing machines, and in the last few years gas stoves had been gaining popularity; household 7, for example, owned one. The stoves used bottled gas, which was regularly brought to the village from the state capital.

Finally, a new form of asset had appeared in the village—the savings account. As table 28 shows, two families had savings accounts on which they were earning annual interest of 4 percent. Another recent innovation had been the savings club. This was started by a local group, and in 1964 some municipal employees, teachers, and others had joined. These clubs had appeared in various parts of the state, particularly among government employees, the one in Tepoztlán being one of the latest to be organized. The club was planning to put its funds in a savings account and disburse its earnings annually. It had also planned to make loans to members at low rates of interest. Since it was just starting, it was difficult to anticipate what effect it might have on the saving habits of the people.

Table 29 shows the annual income of the households. Contrary to what took place in the other three villages, in Tepoztlán the growing of corn as a source of income was losing its dominance; earnings from other crops and income from nonagricultural occupations were becoming more important. Furthermore, more women were entering the labor force. They were getting jobs as teachers, office employees, store clerks, and the like. Households 4, 13, and 14 had women earners.

The difference between income earned from corn and income earned from tomatoes could be marked indeed. In the case of household 13, for example, one hectare of corn produced an income of 2,230 pesos while two hectares of tomatoes produced an income of 14,150 pesos. And it should be added that the difference would have been greater if the use of the modern methods had not sharply increased the corn yield. The head of the household stated that the hectare of corn which in 1963 produced 2,475 kilograms of corn, before modernization only produced 900 kilograms. In similar

TABLE 29

Annual Income, by Principal Sources, of Households
Sampled in Tepoztlán, 1963
(In Current Pesos)

HOUSE-HOLD NUMBER	CORN OUTPUT[a]	OTHER AGRICULTURAL PRODUCTS[b]	ANIMAL PRODUCTS[c]	ARTS AND CRAFTS	OTHER SOURCES	TOTAL EARNED INCOME	PER CAPITA INCOME
1	3,170	250	1,920	....	520[d]	5,860	837
2	....	180	....	....	4,860[e] 260[f]	5,300	757
3	....	....	....	9,360[g]	....	9,360	936
4	2,700	3,310	undet.	....	4,800[h] 1,025[d] 500[i]	12,335	1,541
5	2,160	4,500[j]	200	....	....	6,860	857
6	....	350	1,100	2,600[k]	3,600[e] 200[d]	7,850	2,616
7	3,575	....	730	....	150[d]	4,455	742
8	....	....	....	....	3,450[e]	3,450	862
9	810	300	350	....	6,700[i]	8,160	1,360
10	....	....	550	6,000[g]	....	6,550	1,637
11	7,560	....	undet.	....	undet.	7,560	945
12	1,710	685	400	120[m]	1,170[e]	4,085	2,042
13	2,230	14,150[j]	....	2,400[g]	7,200[e]	25,980	2,598
14	....	....	350	8,650[n]	7,200[e]	16,200	3,240
15	3,420	1,000	undet.	....	1,900[i]	6,320	2,106

[a] Based on an average price of 0.90 pesos per kg. of corn.
[b] Figures include the market value of hog plums, avocados, coffee, and other less important products.
[c] Figures include the value of the production of eggs (0.50 pesos each) and the value of milk sold (2 pesos per liter).
[d] Income from rent of oxen or from rent of land.
[e] Wages.
[f] Gifts.
[g] Wages earned in masonry work.
[h] Salary.
[i] Income from sale of animals.
[j] Value of tomato crop.
[k] Income from shoemaking.
[l] Includes wages in the amount of 4,100 pesos, and profits from the sale of soft drinks in the amount of 2,600 pesos.
[m] Income from manufacture of agricultural implements.
[n] Includes wages of one earner as butcher in the amount of 3,650 pesos, and wages of another earner as mason in the amount of 5,000 pesos.

fashion, through the use of modern practices other farmers had more than doubled their corn yields.[7]

The growing of tomatoes could be profitable indeed, but it was not riskless. First there was the question of the delicate nature of the crop, for unless proper care and know-how were applied, the output, if any, was likely to be small. Then, the wholesale price was subject to extreme fluctuations which also created risks. Some growers reported that there had been times when a 30-kilogram box of tomatoes had sold for 4 pesos, a price which hardly covered the cost of transportation to Mexico City, the market where the bulk of the tomato output was sold. At other times, however, the price had reached 110 pesos the box.

Household 13 produced over 330 boxes of tomatoes which it sold at an average price of 42.50 pesos each. This price was of course high enough to allow a substantial profit, and if a man was lucky enough to sell his crop at such a price, in two or three years he could accumulate enough earnings to start buying his own mechanized equipment. Low prices, on the other hand, could mean a considerable loss not only in terms of labor but of money because the growing of tomatoes required sizeable expenditures for fertilizer, insecticides, hire of tractors and laborers, and in some instances, rent of land.[8] Most of these costs had to be incurred well in advance of the harvest so that the cultivation of one hectare alone required about 3,000–4,000 pesos of ready cash and in some cases even more.

Needless to say, the tomato prices were set by the wholesale market in Mexico City. At times wholesalers contracted with a grower the outright purchase of the tomato field. The head of household 5 entered into this type of contract. He sold the output of his tomato field (0.4 ha.) in advance for the sum of 4,500 pesos. Some wholesalers would go as far as to advance

7. On the basis of the sample the average corn yield was found to be 1,624 kg. per ha., this figure being based on the total amount of land dedicated to corn (18.7 ha.) and the total output (30,375 kg.).
8. Two farmers not included in the sample informed the author that low tomato prices caused them each a loss of 6,000 pesos in 1963.

funds (interest free) to the growers in exchange for the commitment on the sale of the crop. As mentioned above, financial losses could also occur through lack of knowledge and skill, particularly in connection with pest control and the proper use of insecticides. In 1963 the head of household 11 planted a tomato plot (0.3 ha. in size) and lost many plants to pests even though he used fumigation. He barely recouped his expenses.

The agricultural cycle showed some variations. Some farmers planted tomatoes during the rainy (or regular) season, others planted them after the rainy season, still others planted corn during the rainy season and tomatoes immediately thereafter, and those who had enough land planted both corn and tomatoes during the rainy season. The crops that were rotated with corn were watermelons, peanuts, squash, and gladiolas—the latter two, incidentally, were considered almost as profitable as tomatoes.

As mentioned earlier, many farmers continued to grow corn because they enjoyed it, others did it because they lacked the initial capital required to plant squash, tomatoes, or gladiolas, and others did it for safety reasons. If a new crop ran into the problem of low prices, the corn assured, as a minimum, the household's major food requirement.

The fifth and sixth columns of table 29 show that income from nonagricultural occupations and from wages and salaries was as important and as common as income from agriculture. The "total earned income" column shows that the earnings of many households were relatively high, although the large size of the families made the per capita income low in some cases. The average per capita income of the households sampled was 1,432 pesos.

In table 30 the principal annual living expenditures of the Tepoztecan households are presented. The data bring out once more the importance of food expenditures. These, on the average, amounted to between 10 and 15 pesos per day. The expenditures on clothing were smaller, but compared to the corresponding expenditures of the other villages they

TABLE 30

Principal Annual Living Expenditures of Households

Sampled in Tepoztlán, 1963

(In Current Pesos)

HOUSE-HOLD NUMBER	FOOD	CLOTHING	UTILITIES	OTHER	TOTAL
1	3,300	700	120[a]	600[b]	5,720
				1,000[c]	
2	3,390	600	120[a]	....	4,110
3	5,200	1,000	100[d]	1,000[e]	8,100
				800[f]	
4	3,900	1,300	....	....	5,200
5	3,100	700	130[d]	400[e]	4,330
6	3,650	600	20[d]	105[e]	4,375
7	3,650	1,000	645[g]	....	5,295
8	2,550	300	160[h]	....	3,010
9	5,500	600	110[d]	1,500[f]	7,710
10	4,380	400	95[d]	2,000[e]	6,875
11	undet.	undet.	undet.	undet.	5,500[i]
12	2,200	300	....	....	2,500
13	undet.	undet.	undet.	undet.	6,500[i]
14	5,110	1,200	150[d]	....	6,460
15	3,250	500	240[h]	2,000[f]	5,990

[a] Cost of water service.
[b] Purchase of animals.
[c] House repairs and improvements.
[d] Cost of electricity.
[e] School expenditures.
[f] Medical expenditures.
[g] Includes expenditures on water, electricity, and gas.
[h] Cost of electricity and water service.
[i] Estimate.

were higher and showed more variation, reflecting perhaps the higher developmental level of the community.

Expenditures for electricity were common to most households. Of the households sampled only two lacked electric service. A few households had water service, for which they paid a charge of 10 pesos per month. Other expenditures included house repairs and improvements, medical services, and costs of education.

TABLE 31

Principal Annual Occupational Expenditures of Households

Sampled in Tepoztlán, 1963

(In Current Pesos)

HOUSE-HOLD NUM-BER	HIRE OF LABOR AND EQUIP-MENT	SEED AND ANIMAL FEED	CAPI-TAL AND OTHER	TOTAL OCCUPA-TIONAL EXPENDI-TURES	TOTAL LIVING AND OCCUPA-TIONAL EXPENDI-TURES[a]	AVAILABLE FOR OTHER EXPENDI-TURES AND SAVINGS[b]
1	. . . .	990	160[c] 20[d]	1,170	6,890	−1,030
2	. . . .	500	undet.	500	4,610	690
3	. . . .	. . . .	. . . .	. . . .	8,100	1,260
4	250[e] 265[f]	500	190[c] 380[d]	1,585	6,785	5,550
5	160[e] 50[f] 35[h]	195	2,770[g]	3,210	7,540	−680
6	. . . .	1,290	65[d]	1,355	5,730	2,120
7	640[e] 555[f]	875	320[c] 35[d]	2,425	7,720	−3,265
8	. . . .	. . . .	. . . .	. . . .	3,010	440
9	20[e] 105[f] 180[h]	310	40[c]	655	8,365	−205
10	. . . .	400	undet.	400	7,275	−725
11	. . . .	975	2,580[i]	3,555	9,055	−1,495
12	75[e] 120[h]	300	80[c] 520[j]	1,095	3,595	490
13	260[e] 180[f] 90[h]	675	40[d] 1,265[k] 1,295[l]	3,805	10,305	15,675
14	. . . .	475	65[d] 750[l]	1,290	7,750	8,450
15	140[e] 960[f] 1,050[h]	undet.	undet.	2,150	8,140	−1,820

To conclude the survey of Tepoztlán, table 31 lists the main occupational expenditures. The second column of the table shows that many farmers incurred expenses in the hire of equipment and labor. The latter was usually obtained at wages varying from 10 to 12 pesos per day, and a tractor could be hired to plow one hectare of land for 150 pesos. Land could be rented, but since it was in short supply it was not always possible to do so. In 1963 two of the households interviewed (5 and 12) rented land.

Expenditures on corn seed were small, amounting in most cases to some 13 pesos per hectare. Animal feed represented a larger expenditure, although as in the other villages, most of the feed was obtained from the corn stalks and husks. The fourth column shows that practically all those who farmed purchased fertilizers. Another expenditure shown by this column is tax on land and real estate, which also was common to many households.

According to the last column of table 31, seven households had deficits. In most cases these had been caused by special circumstances. Household 1 purchased two hogs for 600 pesos and had house repairs in the amount of 1,000 pesos, household 7 purchased a bull for 1,500 pesos, household 9 had medical expenditures of 1,500 pesos, household 10 had house repairs of 2,000 pesos, household 11 purchased an ox for 2,100 pesos, and household 15 had medical expenses amounting to 2,000 pesos. Some of these deficits, however, were more

---

[a] Total occupational expenditures of fifth column plus last column of table 30.
[b] Total living and occupational expenditures deducted from total earned income (seventh column) of table 29.
[c] Cost of fertilizers.
[d] Taxes.
[e] Hire of tractors and trucks.
[f] Hire of labor.
[g] Includes expenditures on the tomato crop (1,600 pesos), cost of fertilizers (240 pesos), taxes (30 pesos), and rent of land (900 pesos).
[h] Hire of oxen.
[i] Includes purchase of an ox (2,100 pesos), and cost of fertilizers (480 pesos).
[j] Rent of land.
[k] Cost (undetermined) of fertilizer and insecticides.
[l] Commuting cost (by bus).

apparent than real because some households had earnings that were not included as part of their income. For instance, the head of household 7 received financial help from a son who was a cattle rancher, and household 15 had sizeable earnings from the sale of milk and cheese, but in both cases this income was not recorded.

Five households had to incur debts to meet their expenditures. Household 2 borrowed small sums from relatives, the head of household 4 because of considerable legal expenditures had had a loan outstanding in 1963 for five months on which he had paid interest of 1.6 percent per month, household 8 borrowed 350 pesos free of charge for sundry purposes, household 9 had construction costs and medical expenditures for a child with polio,[9] and household 10 borrowed 800 pesos at an interest of 8 percent a year. Of the other households, eight had incomes large enough to leave ample margin for other expenditures and savings.

Table 32 gives some summary data of the household survey. The figures shown by table 32 are self-explanatory. They summarize some of the most important findings of the field survey, and use will be made of them in the analysis to follow. At this point attention may be called to the per capita income figures. Since Tepoztlán was the largest and most developed village, it might have been expected to have the largest per capita income; but instead the table shows it ranking third. This may be due to the nonrandom nature of the samples. Tepoztlán's sample did not include high income households, but Mitla's and Chan Kom's did. In the case of the two latter villages, the inclusion of some wealthy mer-

9. The head of household 9 and his wife had been married for about ten years. During this time they had been members of a savings group comprised of eleven families. Every week each family put 50 pesos in a savings pool; then, on a rotating basis each family received the proceeds when its turn came. Hence, every eleven weeks a family received 550 pesos. The man's wife said that this method facilitated the accumulation of savings and that these were mainly used for major purchases.

TABLE 32

Summary Findings of the Household Survey, 1963

VILLAGE	AVERAGE SIZE OF HOUSE-HOLD	AVER-AGE PER CAPITA INCOME (pesos)	NONAGRI-CULTURAL INCOME (%)[a]	AVERAGE CORN YIELD[b]	AVERAGE SIZE OF AGRICUL-TURAL PLOT (ha.)[e]	AVERAGE CORN OUTPUT PER HOUSE-HOLD (kg.)	DEFICIT HOUSE-HOLDS (%)[d]
Mitla	5.5	1,931	60	537	5.6	2,285	50
Chan Kom	6.5	1,664	66	471	9.0	4,246	30
Soteapan[e]	8.3	801	26	737	3.7	2,456	66
Tepoztlán	6.0	1,432	60	1,624	2.4	3,375	47
All four	6.25	1,526	60	659	4.8	3,284	44

[a] Sum of columns 4, 5, and 6 of the income tables divided by the sum of column 7 (total earned income), times 100.
[b] Corn output in kilograms divided by number of hectares cultivated.
[e] Total number of hectares planted with corn divided by number of house-holds engaged in its cultivation.
[d] Number of households shown with a negative sign in column 5 of the occu-pational expenditures tables divided by the total of households, times 100.
[e] Small sample (three households); the data reflect a period of transition.

chants with relatively large incomes tended to pull the average upward.

The fourth column shows that the income earned in non-agricultural occupations could be important indeed. Here again, since Tepoztlán's nonagricultural sector was the largest, it may be surprising to see that the percentage of non-agricultural income does not reflect the importance of the nonagricultural sector; however, this may be due once more to the nonrandom character of the sample. The large earnings from commerce of two of Chan Kom's households account in large measure for this village's high percentage of nonagricultural income, but this does not mean of course that Chan Kom's nonagricultural sector was nearly as important as Tepoztlán's. In any case the nonagricultural earnings for the average of the four villages outranked in importance the earnings from agriculture.

The fifth column shows the average corn yields, and in this

instance there can be no doubt about Tepoztlán's superior performance. This, as may be surmised, was due to the modernization process. Before the latter took place, Tepoztlán's corn yield was probably not much different from the 1963 corn yield of the other villages. As far as average size of agricultural plots is concerned, there is little question that if all the villages had matched Tepoztlán's productivity, the amount of land would have been adequate to produce corn in much larger quantities than those needed for family consumption. Inequality in the distribution aside, the average plot sizes do not seem unduly small. The rather large size of Chan Kom's average plot is explained by the availability of land. As mentioned before, the size of the plot in this village was limited not by the supply of land but by labor and capital.

It was fortunate that in Chan Kom a man was allowed to cultivate as much land as he was able, because this permitted him to offset the effects of decreasing yields and increasing population. The land had become less productive, but the plots had become larger and the output had actually increased. It may be recalled that Steggerda found that in the thirties the average amount of corn produced by a household of 5 persons was approximately 2,982 kilograms, grown on an average plot of some 4.8 hectares.[10] This is to be compared with a 1963 average output of 4,246 kilograms of corn grown by a larger household—with an average size of 6.5— on 9 hectares of land. The other figures of the seventh column of the table are the corresponding corn production averages for the other villages. It may be observed that in spite of its high yield Tepoztlán did not produce, on the average, as much corn as Chan Kom did, but this simply reflects the diminished relative importance of corn in the former village. The last column of the table shows the percentage of deficit

10. See chapter 2.

households. An explanation of these deficits has already been given in the discussion of the households' occupational expenditures and, therefore, further comments are postponed until the next and concluding chapter.

Before bringing the survey of rural households to a close it may be of interest to consider the significance of the expenditure data in relation to what is generally known about family consumption expenditures. The first item worthy of attention are the sums spent on food (see tables 15, 20, 25, and 30), which may seem unduly large. Taking the living expenditures of the Chan Kom households (table 20) as an example, it can be verified that food accounts for 76.3 percent of the total, clothing for 7.31 percent, and the "other" category for some 16.37 percent. It is obvious that the food expenditure represents a large proportion of the total expenditure; however, these data do not include items commonly reckoned as part of family consumption, such as rent, fuel, electricity, and water. Had imputations been made for these items, and also for a variety of goods freely provided by the environment, the food share would have been smaller.

It may also be noted that the expenditure pattern of a community like Chan Kom tends to be narrow. Clothing is simple, expenditures on services such as medical care, transportation, entertainment, and education are small, and therefore food becomes the predominant item of expenditure. Furthermore, most families combine consumption and business expenditures since each farmer is both a consumer and an entrepreneur. Since the expenditure pattern is affected by this dual apportionment, the breakdown of the expenditures ought to be based on the total expenditure of the household. Thus, if the occupational expenditures are combined with the living expenditures to arrive at a combined total, it can be found that food now represents 55.50 percent of the total expenditure, clothing 5.32 percent, other living expenditures 11.91 percent, and occupational expenditures

27.26 percent. Thus the food share reaches a reasonable level.[11]

Taking the consumption shares with respect to income, food is 32.77 percent of total earned income,[12] clothing 3.14 percent, other living expenditures 7.03 percent, occupational expenditures 16.09 percent, available for other expenditures and savings 40.95 percent. The size of the last percentage is surprising indeed, because even though it may include expenditures not shown by tables 20 and 21, it nevertheless allows a rather large margin for savings. A correspondingly high percentage, moreover, can also be found for the other villages: Soteapan's is 22.25 percent, Mitla's is 18.37 percent, and Tepoztlán's is 19.53 percent.

A survey of rural households with which to compare the above results was not available to the author; however, in 1960, Mexico's Ministry of Industry and Commerce conducted an income and expenditure sample survey of the sixteen largest cities in the country and included in the sample was the city of Mérida, Chan Kom's state capital.[13] The urban nature of this survey notwithstanding, its findings are not drastically different from those mentioned above for Chan Kom. In the Mérida survey, food represents 52.72 percent of the total monthly expenditures, housing 11.66 percent, clothing 9.14 percent, and other expenditures 26.48 percent.[14] Thus Mérida's food share is somewhat lower than Chan Kom's, but the difference is rather small and can perhaps be explained by the difference in average household size: 5.2

11. See United Nations, Department of Economics and Social Affairs, *Statistical Yearbook 1963* (New York, 1964), table 171, p. 519. For comparison, the food, beverages, and tobacco percentages of this publication should be combined since the food percentage for Chan Kom includes all three items. See also H. S. Houthakker, "An International Comparison of Household Expenditure Patterns, Commemorating the Centenary of Engel's Law," *Econometrica* 25, no. 4 (October 1957): table 4, pp. 548-49.

12. Total earned income is given by the sum of the seventh column of table 19.

13. *Las 16 ciudades principales de la República Mexicana, ingresos y egresos familiares, 1960* (Mexico: Secretaría de Industria y Comercio, Departamento de Muestreo, 1962). The survey was carried out from August to December, 1960. The expenditures are given on a monthly basis.

14. Ibid., table 1, p. 159. The size of the Mérida sample was 512.

persons for Mérida in contrast to 6.5 persons for Chan Kom.

It is worth adding that the breakdown of Mérida's household expenditures by income class tends to follow Engel's law: in the next to the lowest income class the food share accounts for 50.31 percent of total income, whereas in the highest income class it accounts for only 25.20 percent.[15] Hence, Chan Kom with a corresponding figure of 32.77 percent has a smaller food share than some of the low-income households of Mérida.

In the urban study the data are pooled to arrive at average expenditure percentages for the sixteen cities with the following results: food represents 41.69 percent of total expenditures; housing (including rent, electricity, fuel, and telephone) 14.64 percent; clothing 7.80 percent; entertainment 2.58 percent; servants 2.35 percent; taxes 3.19 percent; durables 8.86 percent; investments (including purchases of real estate, stocks, bonds, and savings accounts) 1.97 percent; and other 18.92 percent.[16] The expenditures amount to 78.46 percent of income and the average size of the household is 5.2. A breakdown of total expenditures by the per capita income of the cities also tends to follow Engel's law. Tijuana, which with a monthly per capita income of 539 pesos is the richest city in Mexico, shows a food expenditure amounting to 36 percent of total expenditures; whereas Morelia, which ranks next to the poorest city with a monthly per capita income of 222 pesos, has a corresponding figure of 55 percent.

If for purposes of comparison the villages' total expenditures are similarly pooled, it is found that the average food expenditure is 51.76 percent of total expenditures, clothing 7.90 percent, other living expenditures 10.45 percent, and occupational expenditures 23.17 percent.[17] When compared to the average food share of the cities, that of the villages is

15. Ibid., table 19, p. 173.
16. Ibid., table 1, p. 29.
17. Due to the fact that three households (household 4 in table 15 and households 11 and 13 in table 30) do not have their total living expenditures broken down, these percentages contain an error of 6.7 percent, distributed among food, clothing, and other living expenditures.

somewhat higher, but as table 32 shows, the average village household has 6.25 persons whereas the cities have 5.2 persons on the average. Thus, household size may be partly responsible for the difference. On the whole the expenditures of the village households seem reasonable.

6

The Traditional Sector
and National Growth

The three decades of village history just reviewed attest to a record of genuine growth. There can be little question that by 1964 the villages had come a long way from where they were in the early thirties. Through a series of improvements, public and private alike, they achieved a significant betterment of their condition. In education, communications, medical care, economic diversification, and consumption—in sum, in important and diverse areas—many changes give evidence of their accomplishments. Contrary to the popular notions, neither stagnation nor lack of interest have characterized them. For the truth is that the villages have not been mere bystanders passively contemplating outside events. Instead, they have been active promoters and development-seekers, very much interested in working toward a better life.

That the villages moved ahead is something that few would deny. But even if they had done nothing more than to maintain their 1930 standard of living, there would still be reason to question whether they had been stagnant. For if a traditional society, in spite of such problems as setbacks imposed by nature (ranging all the way from pests to drought), lack of technical know-how, population increases, and unfavorable outside market and nonmarket conditions, is at least able to hold its ground—in terms of, say, output per head or income per head—one would assume that a larger output must have been produced or else the maintenance of the same standard of living would not have been possible.

If it be granted, then, that the economic growth of the villages can be taken as fact, the question is what factors have been behind this growth? And conversely, what factors have tended to retard it? These questions merit careful consideration, but before some answers are suggested a word about the character of the villages. It may be wondered whether the four villages are typical, in the sense of representing the sort of rural community that one is likely to find throughout Mexico. It may be asked whether archeological sites, the YMCA, and movie companies are commonplace in rural communities, and whether outside government aid is usually extended in the manner indicated in chapters 4 and 5, or whether this aid goes to some villages more than to others because they are better known or are important for some other reason.

So far as archeological sites are concerned, it is true that sites ranking with Mitla's are not found in many places; the ruins at Mitla are too unusual and important for that. Tepoztlán's archeological site does not have the same importance, but it adds attraction to the village. Chan Kom does not have one, but of course it is not far from famous Chichén Itzá, and Yucatán has such extensive archeological areas that it would not be surprising if a site existed closer to the village. Soteapan, to the author's knowledge, has no such site.

Regarding the YMCA, all that can be said is that its operations in Tepoztlán were unique. It had not been the YMCA's practice to go into one community after another organizing programs of rural development. Insofar as the third item is concerned, the presence of movie companies, up until 1964 this had been restricted to Tepoztlán.

The possibility of government aid being influenced by the importance (archeological or otherwise) of the villages seems to apply in the case of Mitla, so far as state aid is concerned. The state government perhaps has been interested not so much in Mitla's having electricity or an adequate water system but in maintaining adequate communication with its ruins. In the case of Tepoztlán it is difficult to say whether when President Cárdenas granted federal aid for the first major project—the road to Cuernavaca—he was influenced by the importance of Tepoztlán or by the insistent requests of the villagers. At the time Tepoztlán already had communication by rail, which provided easier access to the archeological site than any road has done since. Soteapan and Chan Kom have not been important enough to warrant preferential treatment.

In light of the preceding discussion, what can be concluded about the typicality of the four villages? First, that although some of the factors mentioned may have been present in some villages but not in others, they are not necessarily significant, and second, that other elements can be identified as being more closely related to the villages' growth. What these other elements are can be made clear by turning now to the factors that explain the three decades of rural progress.

The first factor that emerges—in all likelihood the most important one—is that growth started from within. The villagers were not told that they had to improve; they undertook reforms and built schools and roads because they desired to do so. The villages' economic growth has been growth in the Schumpeterian sense: it was not forced upon them from without but arose by its own initiative from within. Nobody would deny the importance of outside factors, such as government aid, but even in this case it was the villagers who asked, not the government that offered. Except in land redistribution, it was the villagers who took the initiative. They were the ones who exercised motivation, and without it no measure of progress would have been likely.

This motivation manifested itself in the leadership that some individuals exercised and also in the cooperation with which the people responded to that leadership. Examining the role of leadership first, it appears that all the villages had community-oriented leaders who assumed responsibility for initiating public projects. Whether in road construction, introduction of electricity, procurement of outside assistance, or other projects, it is possible to trace the original efforts to a few individuals who were willing to take the initiative. To mention again the case of Tepoztlán's first road, the initial planning and the solicitations of aid were the work of local leaders. Chan Kom has been host to many outsiders from whom the people have received encouragement and new ideas, but the original contacts, starting with the first encounter with the American anthropologists at Chichén Itzá, were initiated by the Chan Kom leaders. Other examples could be cited, but it seems sufficiently clear that directly in some cases, indirectly in others, indigenous leadership has been responsible for much of the developmental action.

Local leadership has of course varied from village to village. Chan Kom is the place, perhaps, where it can be seen most clearly at work. Such important advances as the attainment of municipal status, the relatively large ejido grants, the construction of public buildings, and the enlistment of outside aid for electrification have all been the work of strong leaders who have given priority to the welfare of their community. Such leadership has tended to offset the growth-limiting effect of a rather meager physical environment. Compared to Chan Kom, Soteapan has better land; it has mountain streams and areas fit for the cultivation of important cash crops. But leadership and a sympathetic attitude toward material success do not seem as prevalent as in Chan Kom, which may be one of the reasons why, in spite of a richer endowment, Soteapan seems to have a slower rate of progress.

The second factor mentioned above is the cooperation which the people have given to their leaders. This has consisted first and foremost of communal labor, supplemented by monetary and nonmonetary contributions. Communal labor is an ancient practice, but contrary to other legacies of the past, it has been a growth factor that has served to activate a resource found in all the villages, namely, manpower.

Through the use of communal labor, activities ranging from the cultivation of public lands to the administration of local government were carried out, thus it effectively functioned as a system of taxation. Communal labor had an opportunity cost. It meant absence from the cornfield or disruption of other activities for a few hours, or even days. On the whole, however, it seemed to be beneficial. A man usually found a relative or friend to look after his plot and the community got the benefit of his work. Unfortunately, as mentioned in the case of Tepoztlán, communal labor may be declining in importance and tending to disappear. This means that greater reliance will have to be placed either on taxes, on special assessments, or on some other form of public contribution.

A further aspect of the endogenous nature of the villages' growth is the receptivity of the people to new techniques. It was mentioned that in Tepoztlán there had been an increased interchange with outsiders and that the visits of agronomists, for instance, had been sought and welcomed, particularly when difficulties arose with the new crops. The people showed willingness to learn new techniques and, in the main, there seemed to be no distrust toward the visiting technicians.

This willingness, however, had developed over a number of years. The presence of tourists had been a feature of village life dating from the twenties. Later, in the early forties, Tepoztlán was exposed to a cultural mission sent by the federal government. This mission, like the one that visited Chan Kom at about the same time, taught the people crafts, home improvement techniques, and promoted sports and various cultural activities. Also dating from that time, as already mentioned, were the activities of the YMCA along similar lines. In sum, Tepoztlán has had a long and continuous exposure to outsiders, and this may account in part for the receptivity of the people to new techniques. Soteapan, in contrast, has lacked a similar exposure and its degree of receptivity appeared to be lower. In any case, strangers seemed to be less welcome in Soteapan than in Tepoztlán.

Whether many years must pass before a traditional society becomes receptive to new techniques is a question that cannot be answered by the study of the four villages. For if Soteapan, whether due to isolation or for some other reason, showed less receptivity than Tepoztlán, Chan Kom illustrates that isolated communities can be highly receptive. The people of the latter village had always shown interest in new ideas and had always welcomed outsiders, national and foreign alike. Therefore if in 1964 the village was characterized by a low technological level, it was not because the people opposed technological know-how but because the latter had not been applied systematically.

The accumulation of savings is the next factor behind the villages' progress. Contrary to the propositions that identify traditional societies with destitution and inability to save, the record in this case demonstrates that saving took place in the villages and that frequently the sums saved were relatively large. The contributions made by Mitla and Tepoztlán for the introduction of electricity and for the water systems reached sizeable amounts. Then, as explained in chapter 3, the taxes effectively paid by the villagers were also rather large, both in an absolute and in a relative sense. It should be made clear, however, that in spite of the fact that the sums collected were large they did not place undue hardships on the people, nor did they impair their health or drastically lower their standard of living. Indeed, it is unlikely that these taxes represented the maximum possible amount that the villagers could pay.

As might be suspected, public funds were not always used for material improvements. On occasion sums were collected to pay for celebrations and feasts. These ranged from national holidays to the feast in honor of the local patron saint and were usually accompanied by considerable expenditures for entertainment. The importance of some of these celebrations appeared to be on the wane. In Chan Kom, where material success was always considered a worthwhile goal, the people had purposely reduced the number of village feasts. Traditionally they used to hold a religious celebration every year, but aware of the costs and the material alternatives that they had to forgo, they had changed it to once every two years. In Tepoztlán and Mitla certain traditional feasts were also on the wane, although many others remained.

At the household level the field surveys show that most households were also able to save.[1] With the exception of Soteapan, where unusual conditions prevailed, the number of households with recorded deficits in each village represented a minority of those sampled. The actual number of deficits, moreover, was smaller than that shown by the tables, because in a number of instances the income recorded was smaller than the true income. Furthermore, in some cases deficits were related to disbursement of accumulated savings. When a man purchased cattle or built a new house, he may actually have been spending money previously saved. Since in the year of the expenditure his outgo exceeded his income, he of course appeared with a deficit in the table; an actual deficit, however, probably did not occur. Proof of this is given by the fact that whereas the total number of deficits for the thirty-six households sampled was sixteen, the number of households which actually had to borrow money to make up deficits was only four. Three more households did some borrowing; but the sums involved were small, they were obtained free of interest, and the period of the loan was quite short. This means that actual deficits were the exception rather than the rule and that when they occurred they were met by dissaving rather than borrowing; a circumstance further attesting to the existence of household savings. Of course even in the absence of the household income and expenditure figures, the fact that the villagers improved their homes, acquired productive goods, purchased durables and the like was a strong indication of the existence of savings.

1. See the tables on occupational expenditures and the last column of table 32. See also the savings rates given at the end of chapter 5.

Saving presented one difficulty: more often than not it had to be done irregularly. The reason was that a great share of the income was supplied by agriculture, which depended on weather conditions. Good weather meant a good crop and an income large enough to exceed expenditures; poor weather had the opposite effect. It is interesting to note in this respect that in Tepoztlán, where the relative importance of nonagricultural occupations was increasing, saving was becoming institutionalized through savings clubs and bank savings accounts, and that teachers, public employees, clerks, and other nonfarm workers had been the first to join.

Outside governmental action is the next factor that has been important for the growth of the villages. It was governmental action, federal and state in some cases or one of them alone in others, that produced land redistribution under the agrarian reform, contributions to public projects, aid for the operation of schools, provision of health services, etc. It is true that, as mentioned above, government aid was not volunteered. Outside governmental agencies did not come to the four villages with planned programs of rural development. In any event, when big projects were at stake, government aid supplied the missing ingredient that made them possible.

Also contributing to the growth of the villages have been the improvements in education. The elimination of many traditional occupations, the discovery of new ones, the broadening of the nonagricultural sector, the growing participation of women in the labor force, the tendency toward economically oriented behavior, and the adoption of such practices as institutionalized methods of saving—all were probably due in some way to the influence of education. These effects were more or less immediate; the full impact of education, however, was yet to be felt. It was previously mentioned that in 1964 Tepoztlán had at last a well-educated professional as president, but what effect or influence he—and others like him—would have on advancing the economic cause of the communities was still unknown.

It is sometimes asked whether education precedes or whether it follows economic growth. Some economists suggest that instead of being a precondition it is a concomitant of growth. A recent study offers some evidence in support of the proposition that education does have an effect on economic growth; the effect, however, is delayed and not felt for a period of ten to twenty years.[2] In this regard the experience of the villages demonstrates on the one hand that illiterates have promoted economic growth (and, it may be added, progress in education) and on the other that education and growth seem to have kept pace with each other. Something else is shown by the villages' experience and that is the need for complementary growth in occupational opportunities. Elementary education, vocational training, and high school education have been made realities, but they have led to a steady outflow of educated young people. Some of them had to leave to go to another school, but some of them left because there were no jobs for lathe operators or mechanics in the village. Education alone is not enough; beyond it there must be opportunities for its exercise. After he has been educated a young man needs an occupation in which he can apply his knowledge. If not, looked at from the standpoint of the villages, education leads to a loss.

Besides education, better communication is another factor behind the villages' progress. The opening of roads sparked the expansion of trade, the ownership of vehicles, and activity in transportation. In Tepoztlán shortly after the inauguration of the paved road, bus lines were organized which have been sources of income and employment ever since. Similarly, the purchases of trucks, taxis, and private automobiles owe their increasing popularity to the same factor. Some of the roads, to be sure, have not been professionally engineered and outside observers might even question whether they can properly be called roads, but they opened the door to the outside and exposed the villages to growth-

2. D. C. McClelland, "Does Education Accelerate Economic Growth?" *Economic Development and Cultural Change* 14, no. 3 (April 1966): 257.

promoting influences. After it was reachable Tepoztlán attracted the YMCA, the Boy Scouts, influential friends who were instrumental in the attainment of its goals, and strangers who pioneered its agricultural transformation. Chan Kom built up its hog, cattle, corn, and poultry exports through trade that roads made possible, and the same thing can be said about the other villages.

Improved communications, moreover, also seem to have affected consumption patterns. If in Mitla and Tepoztlán the people appeared more up to date in their clothing, in their household furnishings, and in their personal grooming, it was probably because they had better communications and greater exposure to outside influences. Stronger political links have been fostered in the same manner. The federal government requests an annual municipal report on the output of crops, fruits, livestock, etc., and to the more isolated villages this has caused an increased awareness of the government's existence. In similar fashion, better communications have also facilitated closer relations with the state governments.

The benefits outlined have not accrued to the villages without cost. Roads promoted trade, but they also facilitated the influx of goods which competed against the native industries and which made some crafts disappear. Roads allowed new ideas to flow in, but they also made easy the flight of precious capital: the ambitious and educated village youth. It is true that those who sought higher education of necessity had to leave, the problem is that they failed to return.[3] It may be granted that the villages did not offer opportunities for the practice of some professions, but was their permanent departure inevitable? Were they more useful or productive in the city? Not necessarily, for even professionals themselves admit that some of them would be more useful,

3. It will be recalled that in Tepoztlán in 1964 twelve students expected to receive college degrees, none of whom, so far as the author was able to tell, planned to return.

and incidentally earn more money, if they worked in small towns and even in villages. In the cities a concentration of professionals means competition and modest incomes for many of them.

So much for the factors that have stimulated growth. What can now be said about the obstacles that made this growth difficult? The lack of greater concern by the educated toward their villages already previews the difficulties that the latter faced, but there were others. One that ought to be considered at the outset is natural resources. These for the most part are meager. To wit, Mitla's lands are stony, most of Tepoztlán's lands are mountainous, and the terrain around Chan Kom contains only scattered patches of soil. This for communities that derive a good portion of their livelihood from the land is no small matter. One can agree that it is not resources but what people make of them that counts and that other things are more critical for growth. However, when a society of peasants has to build up the economic infrastructure, diversify its income-producing activities, change attitudes, break down the physical and cultural isolation, etc., meager resources cannot but make the job more difficult. Examples of societies that sit on top of wealth and remain backward, even when they know of it, do not invalidate the argument.

The size of the community itself seems to be another growth-limiting factor. In Chan Kom, for example, the population is so small that there is not much room for specialization or efficient division of labor. Besides farming, every man also engages in housebuilding, toolmaking, and many other nonagricultural tasks, but nobody makes a living from any of these occupations. Contrariwise, in the larger villages a man has the opportunity to become a craftsman or a small businessman and can thereby gain greater benefit to himself and to his community.

Population, of course, plays two opposing roles. In some villages a small population may prevent the efficient utilization of labor, but rapid population increase can have a growth-retarding effect. It is true that some of the villages supported larger populations in the past, but the quality of living is obviously not the same. In Tepoztlán, where the population increase had been coupled to the diversion of land to nonagricultural uses, unemployment was beginning to be a problem. On balance, as mentioned in chapter 3, the villages appear to be population losers and this has tended to reduce the pressure, but they still absorb part of the increase and consequently the population rise has presented some problems.

Agricultural prices can act as a spur to greater output, but they can also have a growth-retarding effect. If prices are high the income received is proportionately high, if prices are low income is low. In the latter case, though, low prices can also cause reductions in output. Examples are provided by the cobweb-like manner in which planting was curtailed in Chan Kom when the corn price fell and by Tepoztlán's neglect of hog plum production to which low prices contributed.[4] Needless to say, as agriculture becomes more commercialized, outside prices will have even greater repercussions on village income and production. Whether the effect is growth or retardation, this is one more risk that the villages will have to accept for becoming more enmeshed with outer markets.

Lack of technical know-how is another factor that has slowed down village progress. Admittedly, the physical environment tends to dictate the use of particular implements and the degree to which they can be replaced by modern ones. Too, the use of primitive tools does not necessarily imply lack of technical know-how, because under some conditions they may be the ones most suitable. In Mitla wooden plows are widely used because the steel ones are continuously

4. In the latter case besides low prices the presence of pests also contributed to the neglect. However, if prices had been high, attempts would probably had been made to restore production.

broken by the rocks buried in the ground, and in Tepoztlán
and Chan Kom the hoe agriculturalists use the digging stick
because it is impossible to use plow and oxen, to say nothing
of tractors. All in all, however, ignorance is still an obstacle
to newer methods and higher outputs.[5] This deficiency,
moreover, has placed the villagers at a disadvantage when
they have had to fight pests, predatory animals, epizootics,
insects, and such. Were it not for the efforts of the federal
government—and of the state governments to a smaller extent—the deficiency in technical knowledge could hamper
the village growth for a long time. In Tepoztlán the services
of government agronomists and other technical advisors were
increasingly being used, but in the other communities there
was practically no outside technical assistance.

Were it asked, incidentally, in what areas could the educated apply their talents, the answer is that bringing technical knowledge to the villages could be one of those areas.
For here motivation, no matter how strong, cannot fill the
vacuum.

There is a growth-retarding factor that can be traced to
personality traits of the people themselves. It consists of old
beliefs and traditions deeply rooted in their character. Nonpecuniary motives are illustrative. Many times opportunities
for profit are forgone either because there is a sentimental
attachment to traditional ways[6] or because business and
pleasure are not clearly separated and the former does not
necessarily take precedence over the latter. Chase made this
clear when he wrote: "The motive of the market as a whole
is not a pecuniary one. People do not go to make a profit;
they go to deliver what they have made, get what they need,

5. In Chan Kom the author asked Mr. Ceme why, since he had a water well
with a pump and sufficient land, he did not grow alfalfa for his animals. He
replied that he would be interested in so doing but he did not know what
alfalfa was.
6. The reader may recall how a sentimental attachment to corn prevented
some farmers in Tepoztlán from switching fully to the new and more profitable crops.

and pass the time of day. The Aztec marriage of market day and holiday has never been dissolved."[7]

It is also likely that on occasion the people are nonpecuniarily oriented without realizing it. For example, the inconsistencies between the money and barter systems in Soteapan, the failure of the people to take advantage of speculation-ripe situations, and the losses sustained by wage earners because of their insistence on being paid in corn rather than in money, all probably escaped their awareness. It seems that at other times people were aware, but they had peculiar reasons for their behavior. Some women in Soteapan did not patronize the corn-grinding mills because they were afraid that people would think they were lazy.[8] In some instances, as Hatch observed, it was stubbornness that kept them from pecuniary gain; in others, the person deliberately restrained his efforts because he thought that it was unwise to be too ambitious; in still others it was pure sentimentalism—as when a man failed to make a profit on the sale of an old horse because he was attached to it.

These nonpecuniary manifestations could not be considered synonymous with irrational behavior, because in the scheme of values of the villages they embodied accepted norms. From a purely economic point of view, however, it is

7. Stuart Chase, *Mexico: A Study of Two Americas* (New York: Macmillan Co., 1931), p. 209. Chase's observation has been confirmed by many visitors to village markets where vendors refuse to hasten their sales on the grounds that if they did they would be left with nothing to sell; to them the market is excitement more than work. Chase gives other examples. He relates, "Not only goods are exchanged, but equally important, news. Stop an Indian on a mountain trail, market-bound with a load of pottery on his back, and offer to buy the lot at his own price. Nine times out of ten he will refuse to sell at any figure. To part with his pots would deprive him of excuse to go to market. Money is but heavy metal; the plaza is colour and news and life" (ibid., p. 134). He also mentions the case of a friend of his who one time doubled the wages of his laborers only to find that they responded by cutting their working time in half. This made necessary a return to the old wage to secure steady labor. Then there was the case of an Indian carpenter who, after doing some work for a woman, deliberately avoided appearing near the woman's house so it would not seem that he was trying to collect his wages (ibid, pp. 221-22).
8. See also Chase, *Mexico,* p. 133.

apparent that they interfered with material achievement and that they kept the peasants from exhibiting all the behavior attributed to *homo oeconomicus*. Fortunately, these values were not powerful enough to obliterate the material interests of the villagers; in addition their hold on the villagers seems to weaken with each new generation.

Besides nonpecuniary motives, certain practices and characteristics peculiar to the four villages can be singled out as tending to retard their development. Among these it is possible to list the social consumption associated with many feasts, rituals, and ancient customs; disdain toward material success; destructive behavior caused by envy; and purchase of assets for reasons of "prestige" rather than for their productive value. The degree of noneconomic behavior varies from village to village, and in the largest one it may be gradually disappearing. Here it can be observed that the farmers who hire a tractor or purchase fertilizers are more conscious of revenue and expenditures and thus act like profit maximizers. The same comment applies to those who go into commerce or who enter nonagricultural activities such as transportation, small scale industry, etc.

The growth-retarding factors mentioned thus far are the most discernible ones, although it also seems that developmental action in one area, unless supported by complementary action in other areas, can lead to unanticipated difficulties. Some theorists may consider this advantageous because attention is drawn to critical points; this may be so, but the unbalances can become chronic and very much inimical to further growth. Attention was called to this problem in the preceding discussion concerning the role of education, and the same problem arises in connection with land reform. A peasant certainly benefits from the ownership of land, but if this is not accompanied by extension services, irrigation, credit, and the like, the benefit is uncertain. In the absence of irrigation or adequate rainfall, a farmer who invests in fertilizer, hire of equipment, etc., can be subject to grave setbacks. The installation of some irrigation facilities would be a great improvement, but they may involve expenditures exceeding the savings of many farmers. Under these conditions, credit facilities could perform a valuable complementary function. There are money lenders in all the villages, but enough examples have been given to show that the interest rates charged can be extremely onerous.

To its credit, the Mexican government has taken action in the areas associated with land reform, but in 1964 there were still many villages where the latter had not gone beyond the land distribution phase. In these circumstances it is easy to understand why so many peasants willingly left their villages to become farm laborers in the United States. In Mitla and Tepoztlán farmers who had become successful despite the vagaries of the weather, when comparing their situation with that of most of their fellow farmers, or when looking back to the years before they achieved success, used an expression to the effect that "to farm with rain is an enterprise of fools." Most peasants seemed to be aware of this but for many there was no choice.

No more need be said at this point about the factors that have aided the villages to grow or about the factors that have made this growth difficult. Few would deny that the villages are traditional yet dynamic, that they may not be modern like the cities but are not stagnant, that they may have a low level of living but are not destitute, that the peasantry may exhibit nonpecuniary motives but is not indolent. Yet there is a gap, the traditional-modern gap that set the tone of the study. For all their dynamism and enterprise the villages still have a long way to go before they begin to catch up with the modern sector, or to put it in another way, before they become integrated into the national economy. Thus the important questions are: What does their growth mean? Where does that growth place them (1) with respect to the nation as a whole and (2) with respect to the sector that has attained a much higher developmental level? These questions could be approached from the point of view of the villages. One may be concerned about what the future holds in store for them, or one may ponder ways they can overcome their difficulties. But a more relevant approach is to examine the questions from the point of view of the country. The concern ought to be not with growth in the traditional sector but with maximum overall growth of the nation. It may be that no maximum overall growth is possible without maximum growth in the traditional sector, but this is precisely the question that needs investigation.

Before pursuing this further, a shift of focus away from the villages may facilitate the ensuing discussion. When considering the problem of the gap, it may be observed that interregional inequalities can be emphasized or deemphasized depending on how regions are delineated. In general the larger the regions involved, the smaller the gap. In other words, the difference in per capita income, for example, tends to be smaller when multistate regions are compared than when the comparison involves single states.[9] The degree of interregional inequality can also be made to vary depending on which regions are defined as poor and which regions are defined as rich. As a practical matter, however, the two sides of the rich-poor dichotomy can be expected to be so well defined as not to make identification a problem.

So far as the unit of comparison is concerned, it seems that it should be possible to use either total income of the areas compared or per capita income, save that the former measure, by not giving weight to population, may yield a less accurate picture of a given situation.[10] Of the two, per capita income is a more meaningful measure, although it should be kept in mind that a region could have a rising per capita income due to emigration and not to a superior economic performance. Of course, even heavy emigration could not

9. For an elaboration of this point see the Appendix, part A.
10. This is elaborated in the Appendix, part B.

prevent a fall of per capita income if a region deteriorated severely.

One more item should be made clear. When comparing the per capita income growth of poor versus rich regions, a distinction needs to be made between absolute and relative gains. Since the growth of different regions will be measured from disparate bases, the percentage increase measured from the smaller base can exceed the percentage increase measured from the larger base. In absolute terms, however, the increment of the larger base will in all likelihood be larger than the increment of the smaller base, even though the relative increases favor the smaller base. Frequently this distinction is not made, and relative changes tend to be confused with absolute changes.

With these preliminaries out of the way it is now possible to go back to the main theme and ask again: What is the significance of the villages' progress? The first step in working toward an answer is to establish how the villages did in relation to the nation at large. If per capita income is to be the measure of regional economic growth, it may be asked whether the villages followed a converging path toward the national average or whether they departed from it.

The question is crucial, and it demands that every possible piece of information—micro and macro—be extracted from the data. There are no statistics that will provide a clear-cut answer; however, fragmentary evidence allows to put a rough picture together. For some of this evidence it is necessary to go outside the villages' experience, but when this is done a consistent pattern emerges that begins to give meaning to their performance. What does this pattern reveal? That the relative growth of the per capita income of the villages is converging toward the national average.

For proof of this proposition it is possible to start with Soteapan's household 1, which both Foster and the author studied.[11] If the value of the three main crops grown (corn,

---

11. Foster also studied household 2, but in 1963 it had such an abnormally low income as to make any comparison meaningless.

coffee, and beans) is taken as the household's income for 1941, it can be determined that the per capita income of the household was 78 pesos. This figure represents approximately 20 percent of the 1941 average per capita income of the entire country.[12] Moving on to 1963 and considering as income the value of the household's output of corn, beans, coffee, fruits, poultry, and eggs, the per capita income of the household amounted to 1,372 pesos, that is, it climbed to approximately 30 percent of the national average.[13] In other words, in a period of twenty-two years the per capita income of this household converged 10 percentage points toward the nation's average income level. This convergence, moreover, took place in spite of the fact that the number of persons in the household increased from four to six. It should also be noted that neither imputations for such things as house rent, water, forest products, communal labor, etc., nor the proceeds from the sale of cattle, are included in the 1963 household income reported above. If the imputations are ignored but the income from cattle is taken into account, the per capita income of the household is that shown by table 24. The figure is 1,905 pesos and represents around 42 percent of the national average. The convergence now reaches 22 percentage points instead of the 10 computed above. Another way of interpreting the results is to note that in current prices the per capita income of the country increased at a rate of 11.9 percent per annum while the per capita income of the household increased at a rate of 15.6 percent per annum. And it must be added that this advance occured in the village that seems to be developing at the slowest pace. In real terms, needless to say, both increases were more modest; but in any case they point toward a greater relative per capita income growth for the household than for the nation as a whole.

12. The percentage is based on a per capita income for Mexico of 381 pesos. This figure is reported in *Mexico 1960: Facts, Figures, Trends* (Mexico: Banco Nacional de Comercio Exterior, 1960).
13. This percentage is based on an estimated per capita income for the country of 4,500 pesos.

A further piece of evidence may be adduced; for this one some of Yates's data may be borrowed.[14] Table 33 presents

TABLE 33

Per Capita GNP, Selected Regions and Mexico, 1940 and 1960

(Constant 1960 Pesos)

	1940	1960	ANNUAL PERCENTAGE INCREASE
Oaxaca	384	1,022	5.0
Federal District	7,850	9,950	1.2
Mexico	1,900	3,800	3.5

SOURCE: Per capita GNP data from Yates *El desarrollo regional de Mexico,* tables 14 and 15, pp. 62-63.

the data. Here the growth rates are expressed not in current but in real terms. Again, there is no question about the superior relative performance of the poor region: Mitla's state of Oaxaca in this instance.[15] Not only does Oaxaca have a greater percentage increase in per capita GNP than the nation as a whole, but its relative performance is also superior to that of the Federal District, the most modern and wealthiest area of the country.

One more piece of evidence taken from Yates can demonstrate the superior growth rate of the poor region. Taking the eight richest states and comparing their combined performance with that of the ten poorest states, Yates found that between 1940 and 1960 while the real per capita GNP of the country increased by 100 percent (see the last row of table 33), that of the eight richest states increased by only 54 percent; the increase of the ten poorest states, however, amounted to 134 percent. This meant that the rich states had an annual rate of growth of per capita GNP of 2 percent, whereas the poor states had a corresponding growth rate of 4.3 percent.

14. P. L. Yates, *El desarrollo regional de Mexico* (Mexico: Banco de Mexico, 1961), pp. 61-62.
15. Oaxaca is considered the poorest state in the country; Mitla is located within its borders.

It can be restated in conclusion that the available data point to a greater relative growth of the less modern regions and, hence, to a narrowing of the interregional disparity. This is a surprising conclusion for it turns out that the sector that allegedly has no savings but has instead labor with zero marginal productivity, etc., is moving ahead at a more rapid pace than the progressive sector. How can this be explained? The factors behind the villages' growth provide some clues, but what can be said about the channels of equalization? Have these mingled with the growth factors so as to bring about convergence of per capita income? If the theory is correct they must have exerted some influence.

Considering the movement of capital first, it appears that in the present instance the direct investment from the rich to the poor regions envisioned by theory did not occur. Yates provides sufficient data to show that for the period 1946–55, for example, the industrial and commercial investment was concentrated in the Federal District.[16] This tendency was offset to some extent by the federal government, because some of its public investments were planned for the rural areas.[17] However, flows of private capital from the modern to the traditional regions seem to have been practically nil.

16. Yates, *El desarrollo regional de Mexico,* tables 24, 25, 28, pp. 79-85. Based on the sum of the gross industrial and commercial investment for the period in question, Yates found that the per capita investment in the Federal District amounted to 6,460 pesos, whereas in Oaxaca it amounted to only 252 pesos. This occurred in spite of the much larger population increase of the Federal District. It may be added, incidentally, that the concentration of investment in the rich areas is not a phenomenon peculiar to Mexico. A similar tendency seems to prevail in Spain and Brazil, for example. In these countries not only does capital fail to move from the rich to the poor regions, but a movement in the opposite direction takes place. See J. R. Lasuen, "Regional Income Inequalities and the Problem of Growth in Spain," *Papers and Proceedings of the Regional Science Association* (1962), pp. 177, 179-80; and S. H. Robock, *Brazil's Developing Northeast: A Study of Regional Planning and Foreign Aid* (Washington, D. C.: Brookings Institution, 1963), pp. 58, 108.

17. When this public investment is taken into account, the total cumulative per capita investment mentioned in the previous footnote appears as follows: Federal District, 7,020 pesos; Oaxaca, 857 pesos.

The experience of the villages reveals that at least until the time of the 1964 field surveys, there had been almost no commercial or industrial investments made by outsiders. In Chan Kom an outsider was allowed to install beehives and he was paying royalties on the honey taken out, and in Tepoztlán there was considerable outside investment in private construction; but a flow of capital for commercial or industrial projects did not take place. The failure of this channel was made the more complete by the fact that there were people in Mitla and Tepoztlán who were beginning to put their savings in banks and insurance companies, institutions which were certain to channel the funds in the direction of the cities.

The movement of goods was more evident in its equalizing role. An increasing volume of trade between all regions seems to have been part of the Mexican development, and the four villages benefited from it. Trade provided opportunities outside agriculture, and the profits derived from it were so attractive that in some cases agriculture was given up entirely. As mentioned above, trade also meant an influx of manufactured products and the disappearance of crafts; nevertheless, on balance there can be little question about the benefits of trade, particularly in view of the importance which exports had for all the villages. It is hardly necessary to repeat that in Mitla many farmers supplemented their agricultural earnings by becoming traveling merchants, that the products of its cottage industries—especially woolen goods—were finding wider markets, that in Tepoztlán agricultural exports had taken on an importance never before even suspected, that even the two more isolated communities derived a good portion of their income from the export of corn, coffee, poultry products, cattle, hogs, etc., and that in general without trade the village development would have been slower.

The movement of labor had seemingly performed an equalizing function—at least on the short run. Some comments have already been made concerning the flight of the educated youth, but the movement of labor in general must now be examined. Of the four villages Chan Kom was the only one receiving immigrant laborers. Some of the younger and more ambitious natives of Chan Kom had moved to Mérida, but in terms of numbers this emigration was offset by the new arrivals. Since these were provided with a house site and farmland, their contribution to output was not made at someone else's expense, and consequently they represented a net gain. Moreover, these immigrant laborers expanded the local market, which meant greater sales for the stores, and they also provided additional hands for communal labor. Hence, although Chan Kom was a net population gainer, this had not affected it adversely; therefore, it can be concluded that its per capita income had been attained through expanded economic activity rather than through loss of population.

The two larger villages, as the discussion of tables 9 and 10 made clear, have been net population losers, and in this situation serious implications arise. Tepoztlán can illustrate the problem. To begin with it should be reiterated that the village's population increase, coupled to the diversion of land to nonagricultural uses, had forced many unskilled laborers to look for employment elsewhere. Some tried to find jobs in other parts of the state, and some went to Mexico City to look for whatever work they could find as wage laborers. Since Tepoztlán offered no work to them, their departure—temporary or permanent—did not represent a significant diminution of the village's product, and the per capita income of those who stayed was in all probability only slightly affected. Had they remained, however, aid would have been required from relatives or friends, and this would definitely have resulted in a lowering of the per capita income. These laborers, moreover, would have also made demands on the available land, and this could have resulted in a deterioration of the man-land ratio by shifting it to less

productive levels, to everyone's disadvantage. As it was, the
merchants lost whatever sales might have been made to them,
and there may have been some changes in the income distribution, but no major economic dislocation was caused
by their emigration.

Since the concern is with overall growth and the equalizing function of the movement of labor, there is something
else to be considered: the effect of the laborers' emigration
on the receiving region. When the emigration was toward
Mexico City or toward the Federal District—and with the
improved communications the journey from Tepoztlán was
easy to make—the migrants came to swell the stream of unskilled laborers who went there for similar reasons.[18] This
rural-urban migration was not of recent origin and had
contributed in large measure to the disproportionate growth
of the Federal District and of the state capitals over the last
twenty years.[19]

The influx of these productive but unskilled laborers could
not but lower the per capita income of the urban areas. This
effect was both immediate and permanent because the immigration was continuous. In all probability once in the city
the newcomers eventually found employment but not without giving rise to staggering social and monetary costs, especially when they went to Mexico City. The social costs included the creation or worsening of slums, congestion, unem-

18. This migration followed the rural-to-urban pattern that seems characteristic of many countries and which has been the subject of numerous economic and sociological studies.
19. N. L. Whetten, in "The Role of the Ejido in Mexican Land Reform,"
(Land Tenure Center, Discussion Paper 3 [Madison: University of Wiscon-
sin, 1963]) gives data related to this phenomenon. He notes that between
1940 and 1960 the total population of Mexico increased 78 percent whereas
that of the state capitals increased 123 percent. Further data on the rural-
urban migration can be found in M. L. Glick, "The Impact of Economic
Development on the Returns to Labor in Agriculture in Mexico," Ph.D. diss.
(University of Chicago, 1963), pp. 57, 62. According to Glick, the migrants were
the most productive laborers. *The Review of the Economic Situation of Mexico*
345, no. 456 (Mexico: Banco Nacional de Mexico) p. 13, shows that in the
1950-60 decade Oaxaca was the second highest net population loser. Out of
every 100 of its migrants, 79.1 were emigrants.

ployment, unrest, delinquency, pollution, etc. It also seems that within the receiving regions the income distribution was made more unequal by this immigration.[20] The monetary costs included huge expenditures for schools, transportation, subsidized housing, medical services, etc., not to mention the mounting sums required to expand other public services such as streets, sewers, and the like. The cost for the provision of water, in particular, had reached in the Federal District inordinate proportions.

This is not all. It should not be thought that the migratory stream consisted of unskilled laborers only. The educated village youth, in a sense, were also part of it. These young people were to be the future leaders, the innovators, the ones who were to further the cause of rural progress. If leadership —as claimed in the present study—has been one of the most important factors in the villages' growth, their loss was one that the villages could hardly afford.

As the migration continues, moreover, the public and private costs reach even more disproportionate levels, and thus it is difficult not to wonder whether the marginal productivity of such heavy expenditures would not be greater if used in less urbanized areas. If present trends continue it is estimated that by 1980 the Mexico City metropolitan area will have 15 million inhabitants, a threefold increase over 1960. Twenty-five percent of the country's population will be concentrated in this area, and the costs implied by such growth will in all likelihood more than triple. It is questionable even today whether the concentration of all types of activities in the capital makes an optimum contribution to national growth, but an uncontrolled further expansion will surely place Mexico City in the ranks of what have been called

20. Yates, *El desarrollo regional de Mexico*, pp. 102-3, notes that in Mexico City the pattern of growth has engendered extremes of wealth and poverty more accentuated than those in any other part of the country. The *Population Bulletin* 20, no. 7 (November 1964), p. 188, reports that an income survey showed that in 1958, 80 percent of the families in the lowest income bracket resided in urban areas.

"parasitic" cities, that is, cities that retard rather than promote the development of the region or country in which they are located.[21] It may seem that these are expressions of undue pessimism, but the fact is that the Mexico City metropolitan area is beginning to rank among the largest in the world, and there is no reason to believe that it will escape the problems that have become characteristic of older metropolitan areas.

Overconcentration and uncontrolled urban expansion are serious indeed; unfortunately, the magnitude of the problem does not seem to have made an impression until the past few years. Hence, it is only recently that valiant efforts have been undertaken to control urban growth. Currently, whether the urban area be the northeastern connurbation of the United States, or Paris, London, or Holland's Rimcity, the problem is not only how to avoid further concentration but how to provide adequate services for the people and businesses already there and how to promote some measure of decentralization.

In their fight against overconcentration of activities, the European countries have used a varied array of policies, tools, measures, controls, etc. The diversion of industry from the overurbanized areas has been promoted by measures which include tax exemptions, low interest loans, government guarantees, accelerated depreciation, land, factories built in advance, freight allowances, etc. For the workers the provisions include training programs, aid in housing, compensation for moving, and other similar measures. Some cities have even introduced restrictions in the issuance of new industrial-building permits.[22]

So serious has the problem of uncontrolled urban growth become that some writers believe that the question of the

21. See B. F. Hoselitz, "Generative and Parasitic Cities," *Economic Development and Cultural Change* 3, no. 3 (April 1955): 278.
22. For a discussion of these measures see U. S., Department of Commerce, Area Redevelopment Administration, *Area Redevelopment Policies in Britain and the Countries of the Common Market* (Washington, D.C., 1965).

optimum size of cities has become an item of the highest priority, and a number of studies have dwelt on the subject.[23] This concern, moreover, has not been focused on the cities of developed countries only. Increasingly some attention has been shifted to the growth-retarding effect of some of the largest cities of emerging countries, where the problem, if anything, has more serious implications.[24] For if the cost of trying to turn the tide in those well-to-do countries that can better afford it is by no means moderate, the cost for an emerging country that lets itself be caught in the same situation can only be disastrous.

In the present instance it is difficult to believe that the interest of the country is served by an intensified urban concentration. The departure of some peasants from the villages might help to improve the man-land ratio; the question is, what are they going to do in the cities? If the marginal productivity of the immigrant laborer were larger in the capital of the country than in the rural areas, the costs and problems of urbanization might be one of the requirements for greater output. The truth is, however, that the city cannot absorb all the incoming labor; therefore if a man had a very low— or even zero—marginal productivity in his village, he carries, as it were, that low productivity with him to his adopted urban environment, especially when he becomes an unemployed slum dweller. Not only that but so far as his individual welfare is concerned, he could find himself in the city at a level of income lower than the one he had before migrating.

Then, there are the villages to consider. It is apparent that,

23. C. E. Browning, "Primate Cities and Related Concepts," in *Urban Systems and Economic Development* (Eugene: University of Oregon, School of Business Administration, 1962), p. 19; United Nations, Department of Economic and Social Affairs, *Economic Survey of Europe in 1954*, (Geneva, 1955) pp. 156-57; R. M. Lillibridge, "Urban Size: An Assessment," *Land Economics* 28, no. 4 (November 1952): 351; Colin Clark, "The Economic Functions of a City in Relation to Its Size," *Econometrica* 13, no. 2 (April 1945): 112-13.
24. See, for example, a discussion of the problems of urban growth in India in J. P. Lewis, *Quiet Crisis in India* (Washington, D. C.: Brookings Institution, 1962), chap. 7.

excepting perhaps Tepoztlán, they do not have redundant agricultural labor and that, as table 32 shows, the average size of the plots cultivated does not reveal a problematic population pressure on the land. In Chan Kom, and traditionally also in Soteapan, there has been no limitation on the size of the plot that a man cultivates. If the families had more earners, larger plots would be cultivated. As a matter of fact, as mentioned at the end of chapter 5, in Chan Kom this is what actually happens. Therefore, labor with zero marginal productivity does not exist. A somewhat similar situation prevails in Mitla, except that here with the soil being poor and lacking irrigation most farmers need to go outside agriculture to make a living.

There are also some externalities that affect all the villages. Chan Kom's history records an incident that can be cited again for purposes of illustration, the emigration of the Protestants. When they departed they took their herds, businesses, knowledge of crafts, etc. They also reduced the size of the local market, eliminated their contribution to communal labor, and even cut the social amenities in half, because with them went one of the two musical groups. Chan Kom has slowly recovered from their departure, but had it not taken place the village's development might have been more remarkable. Hence, as some writers have noted,[25] rural emigration can have depressing effects: skills may be lost, economies of scale may become harder to attain, the social environment may be impoverished, the educated generation may leave a vacuum behind. If those who remain in the villages are the older and less prepared, they may feel less inclined to carry out improvements. As Hathaway points out, "Older farmers are less likely to undertake drastic reorganizations of existing resources themselves because of limits of their physical capabilities and the limited span over which

25. See, for example, Joan Robinson, *Exercises in Economic Analysis* (London: Macmillan & Co., 1962), pp. 8-9.

they might realize returns on large investments."[26] Under extreme conditions an atmosphere can be created "which paralyzes technical and economic progress. In such circumstances the ensuing shortage of agricultural manpower is likely to result in part of the land being taken out of cultivation rather than in mechanization and other labor-saving improvements."[27]

To summarize, while the movement of labor from the villages is partly unavoidable and in some cases may perform a short-run income equalization, it cannot take place without net disadvantages to the cities, to the nation at large, and to the rural areas themselves. In no way do these remarks mean that the educated youth should stay in their villages, or that the national interest lies in promoting "ruralism," or that the nation at large should not have first claim on the educated whether they come from villages or not; this is not the issue. The issue is whether the optimum path of national growth lies in the direction of greater regional unbalance, to which the migration of labor and the undue concentration of professionals in the cities make a contribution.

On a long-run basis it is not clear whether this sort of emigration really acts as an income equalizer. The experience of Mexico, not to mention the experience of other countries,[28] makes such an equalization rather doubtful. Emigration of labor from the traditional areas can seemingly effect a reduction of income differentials, but such reduction is more a consequence of the arithmetical argument than a meaning-

26. D. E. Hathaway, "Migration from Agriculture: The Historical Record and Its Meaning," *Papers and Proceedings of the American Economics Association,* (May 1960), p. 379.
27. United Nations, *Economic Survey of Europe in 1954,* p. 145.
28. A discussion of the failure of out-migration from agriculture to close the gap between farm and nonfarm per capita income in the United States can be found in Hathaway, "Migration from Agriculture," passim. Glick develops the thesis that in Mexico, despite out-migration from agriculture, there has been a widening absolute gap between the earnings and productivity in agriculture and in nonfarm activities. See Glick, "The Impact of Economic Development," chap. 2.

ful economic outcome. Thus if under the conditions stated, the effectiveness of the movement of labor is more apparent than real, the channels of equalization reduce to two: trade, which has been at work, and the movement of capital, which has not.

Does this unimpressive performance of the channels of equalization present a problem? Is it not the case that the villages have been doing well for themselves and that their rate of growth is bringing them closer to the national income level? And if this is so, will they not advance far enough to be able to close the gap? They will, assuming that the growth rates continue; the problem is that it will take too long. The situation is portrayed in table 34.

TABLE 34

Projected Growth of Poor and Rich

Regions of Mexico

REGIONS	PESOS PER CAPITA	ANNUAL RATE OF GROWTH (%)	INITIAL DIFFER-ENCE (pesos)	MAXIMUM DIFFER-ENCE (pesos)	YEAR OF MAXIMUM DIFFER-ENCE	YEARS BEFORE CONVER-GENCE
Rich[a]	7,950[b]	2.0 ⎫				
Poor	1,450[b]	4.3 ⎬	6,500	9,833	2003	76
Rich[c]	9,950[b]	1.2 ⎫				
Poor	1,022[b]	5.0 ⎬	8,928	9,847	1979	61
Rich[d]	4,500[e]	3.5 ⎫				
Poor	1,617[f]	5.0 ⎬	2,883	6,540	2009	71

Source: Data from table 33 and from village surveys.
[a] Rich region: eight richest states. Poor region: ten poorest states.
[b] Per capita GNP, 1960.
[c] Rich region: Federal District. Poor region: state of Oaxaca.
[d] Rich region: Mexico. Poor region: the villages—excluding Soteapan.
[e] Income per capita, 1963.
[f] Average per capita income of three Mexican villages, 1963.

Three alternatives are illustrated by the table. The first alternative involves a comparison between the eight richest states, aggregated to form the rich region, and the ten poorest states, aggregated to form the poor region. The figures of the second column represent GNP per capita for 1960. The growth rates of the third column are real and are based on the trends recorded by Yates for the 1940–60 period. If it is assumed that these rates of growth will continue, it can be seen that in spite of the superior relative performance of the poor region, the absolute difference in per capita income will widen, going from 6,500 pesos in the initial period to a maximum of 9,833 pesos in the year 2003. Thereafter this difference will enter into a narrowing phase, and after thirty-three additional years the per capita GNP of both regions will be equal.

This may seem too pessimistic. What would happen if the growth rates tended to favor the poor region more than in the previous case? The second alternative gives a clue. It involves the same comparison except that in this case the Federal District represents the rich region while the state of Oaxaca represents the poor region.[29] The figures of the second column (again representing GNP per capita for 1960) and the rates of growth are those shown by table 33. As in the first alternative, the absolute difference will increase for a number of years except that, given the much higher growth rate of the poor region, convergence would occur in this instance fifteen years earlier than in the previous case. Convergence, though, would still take sixty-one years.

The third alternative is perhaps the most appropriate to the present study. It involves a comparison between the

29. It is of interest to note that Yates reports a 1960 per capita GNP for Oaxaca of only 1,022 pesos, a figure below the combined per capita income of the three villages (1,617 pesos) and below Mitla's per capita income (1,931 pesos) as shown by table 32. When the Yates's figure is adjusted to reflect national income instead of GNP and to correspond to 1963 instead of 1960, it still comes to only about 1,231 pesos. This means that either Mitla is an above-average village in Oaxaca or that the sample had an upward bias. Or else the difference may be due to the methods of estimation. Since in the calculation of the income of Mitla's households no imputations were made for house rent, water, forest products, communal labor, etc., and since 1963 was a poor year, it does not seem that Mitla's per capita income was overestimated; so as aforementioned, either the Mitla sample is biased upward or else Oaxaca's per capita income is not as low as Yates's data indicate.

country as a whole as the rich region and three of the villages
surveyed as the poor region. For this alternative the first
figure of the second column is the per capita income of the
country in 1963; the second figure is the combined per capita
income of three villages as given by the income tables,
Soteapan being excluded due to its abnormal condition. The
first growth rate is that shown for Mexico by table 33; the
second growth rate is Oaxaca's, and it has here been assigned
to the villages. The growth rates, as with the previous alternatives, are real.

Again, the last column of table 34 shows an interval of
long duration. Using the third alternative, almost three
quarters of a century will have to pass before convergence
occurs. Moreover, this lengthy process would go on despite
the high real rate of growth of 5 percent per year for the
villages.

In no way is it being implied that a development policy
can have full equalization of regional income as its goal;
various factors would invalidate such a policy. Nevertheless,
a reduction of the interregional gap is a realistic goal, and
what is being questioned is whether a national growth rate
of 3.5 percent can be sustained if the growth rate of the poor
regions is not maintained at a higher rate for a good number
of years. It is important to keep in mind that even if the
rates continue, the absolute difference in income will stay
on a widening trend for a period of forty-six years, at which
time it will have reached the sum of 6,540 pesos.[30] This is
critical because after all, as Yates points out, the people of
the poor regions are not going to assess their situation in
terms of their higher relative growth; what will matter is
their actual income in relation to the income of those better
off, and from this point of view what they will face is a

30. The situation of Mexico is not unique. Other countries—some advanced
like the United States, others not so advanced, like Brazil—face a similar
phenomenon. Their poor regions also have higher relative rates of growth
(aided in part by emigration) in spite of which the absolute per capita income
differential continues to rise.

widened differential. Hence, what is required is to make sure that the traditional sector maintains a superior rate of growth for, say, another four decades—a period long enough to at least approach the time when the absolute difference in per capita income will start to decline. Can this be done? Yes, for a while. How? By tapping the so far untapped opportunities for output expansion. The villages have done well, but they have not exhausted all their opportunities. Their available resources can be made to yield a greater product.[31]

A survey of the opportunities available to the villages could constitute a study in itself; however, a few can be mentioned for purposes of illustration. Examining the nonagricultural sector first, it is apparent that there is room for action in the areas of services and small industry. Mitla is surrounded by mountains that contain deposits of colorful green and pink rock which can be used as construction material, but no efforts have been made to start a quarry.[32] Two cottage industries offer room for larger production: liquor distilling and handmade woolen goods. In the case of the latter there seems to be increasing activity, but nevertheless demand appears to exceed production. Then also, Mitla receives many visitors, but their only contribution to the village consists in the payment of two pesos for admission to the archeological site, money which is probably destined for maintenance and keepers' salaries. A restaurant near the site, or a hotel catering to middle-income visitors, or an adequate market place where the villagers could sell their handmade

31. The possibility of obtaining larger outputs from current facilities in other emerging countries has been considered by Wilfred Malenbaum, *Prospects for Indian Development,* (New York: Free Press of Glencoe, 1962), pp. 31-34; W. A. Lewis, "Reflections on South-East Asia," *District Bank Review,* December 1952, p. 6; Arthur Smithies, "Rising Expectations and Economic Development," *Economic Journal* 71, no. 286 (June 1961): 256-57; J. P. Lewis, *Quiet Crisis In India,* pp. 63-66, 143-44; and E. E. Hagen, *On the Theory of Social Change,* (Homewood, Ill.: Dorsey Press, 1962) pp. 48-49.
32. Visitors to the city of Oaxaca can testify to the fact that such rock can be used to construct not only sturdy but beautiful buildings.

goods and souvenirs in greater quantities—any or all of these could be profitable enterprises.

Tepoztlán attracts many tourists, but again no systematic efforts have been made to exploit its full potential for recreation and tourism. There is an expensive hotel in the village, but numerous service facilities for middle-income tourists remain to be developed. An ever increasing amount of motor traffic comes or passes through Tepoztlán, yet there is not even one gasoline station, let alone any kind of facility for the service of motor vehicles—even if it might be only a car washing operation.

The smaller villages also could exploit some nonagricultural activities more effectively. In Chan Kom, for example, the women make and embroider clothing which finds a ready market in Valladolid and Mérida; this, however, is more a hobby than a cottage industry. If flowering plants were systematically grown, the keeping of bees and the sale of honey could become a much more profitable occupation.

There is also a promising, untapped reservoir in the area of human resources. As Schultz indicates, increases in production may depend primarily on the capabilities of the people themselves.[33] Much has been done by communal labor, but it is possible to employ it more efficiently. Some of the communal labor destined for the organization and conduct of festivals could be used for further material improvements. Soteapan could use more leadership and motivation so that success arouses desire for emulation instead of envy. Certain conspicuous consumption could be, if not entirely eliminated, at least reduced. This would free funds for productive investments. There are indications of the willingness of the people to postpone consumption; but if time-preference patterns could be lengthened on the production side, there might be opportunity for introducing crops which, although requiring two or more years to produce a return, would be more profitable.

33. T. W. Schultz, *Transforming Traditional Agriculture,* (New Haven: Yale University Press, 1964), p. 16.

In agriculture there are opportunities for the introduction of more profitable crops which could be grown in addition to corn, or instead of it. In Mitla the land seems to be appropriate for the cultivation of both century plants and castor oil plants. The former would not even have to be exported; if the liquor distilling industry expanded it could absorb greater quantities of them. Alfalfa is already grown in the village but its output could be increased. It seems to be more profitable than corn, and if it became more plentiful it could allow the raising of larger numbers of sheep. The sheep could in turn supply the raw material for a growing woolen goods industry.

In Chan Kom the soil seems to allow the growing of henequen plants, but unfortunately nobody has made an effort to exploit them. Various fruits are grown in the backyards of the houses, but again they are not grown and cared for in a purposeful manner. Soteapan presents a similar picture; various fruits seem to thrive in the region, but they are not properly grown. Yet they could be more profitable than corn.

Finally, even the traditional crops could be produced in larger quantities in all the villages. In Soteapan coffee has been a traditional export crop, but its yield and output could be increased if some of the better wooded areas were dedicated to its cultivation; as it is, they are subject to the slash-and-burn technique, which prevents the full growth of the trees needed for the coffee. The production of the most traditional of all crops, corn, could also be increased. If its cultivation were improved by rotation with other crops or by the use of fertilizers, deep plowing, hybrid seeds, and some irrigation, a doubling of the yield could be within reach of most farmers.

Again, these examples are not exhaustive, but they give an idea of the potential that the villages have for output expansion and further growth. More can also be done in the infrastructure. Chan Kom's experience shows that when people have determination they can build schools with materials wrested from the bush. And if schools can be built by communal action so can other public buildings, water wells, recreation facilities, and roads— not paved, to be sure, but efficient enough to stimulate the flow of trade and new ideas.

Lumpiness of investment, moreover, need not be an obstacle. Tepoztlán had a school system that started at the kindergarten level and ended at the high school level with a number of grammar schools and vocational training in between, but it was not built all at once. In some instances construction literally proceeded one room at a time. Of course it should be realized that the expansion of social overhead capital is not like the building of a factory that becomes a continuous source of employment. Too, social overhead capital may last a long time. As population increases, more of it may become necessary; but its construction will still tend to be discontinuous, and so far as it depends on the communal efforts of the people, it will not of itself directly result in additional income.[34]

It is perhaps apparent that at the heart of the exploitation of the untapped potential lies a process of technological change which, as recent studies show, is of the essence to economic development. At the developmental level of the villages, whether increments of product and income be viewed as a function of the introduction of more profiitable crops or as a function of more efficient methods, the prescription, though simple, is powerful and in any case the same: new and better ways of doing things are needed. Schultz has observed that the agricultural sector of some emerging countries makes efficient use of the factors of production at its disposal, but that the real contribution to growth is not to be expected

34. This argument cannot of course be duplicated if the construction of social overhead capital is financed by the state or federal governments instead of by the work and contributions of the villagers. A general discussion of the possibility of creating infrastructural investment with little or no capital can be found in Robinson, *Exercises in Economic Analysis,* p. 33. See also J. P. Lewis, *Quiet Crisis in India,* p. 61; W. A. Lewis, "Reflections on South-East Asia," p. 7, and *The Theory of Economic Growth,* pp. 219-20.

from an unchanged pattern of factor-use as much as from a transformation that involves the adoption, learning, and use of new factors.[35] In the present case such transformation seems to provide the field of action upon which the further development of the villages ought to be sought. The prescription for action seems entirely feasible if for no other reason that it does not demand massive infusions of outside capital.[36] There are inexpensive innovations available that minimize capital needs. To illustrate, if where conditions permit a plow were used instead of a stick, if animals and fruit trees were properly cared for, if trees were left to provide shade for coffee plants instead of being subject to slash-and-burn, if more coffee or alfalfa were grown instead of corn, or if corn were rotated with other known crops, the innovation would consist, for the most part, of a more efficient use of resources already available. What would be needed in this instance is the spread of knowledge of these methods and the belief in them. It is difficult to say by how much output could be increased, but either more output would be produced from the available resources and from the traditional crops or else more income would be earned from a shift to the more profitable ones.

Would action along the lines suggested be enough? Given the size of the traditional-modern gap and the lengthy process required to close it, can it be hoped that innovations such as those mentioned will make a significant difference? It is quite possible. The doubling of the corn yield alone would be a big step toward the doubling of income. Besides, there are other possibilities still open. These may represent somewhat higher costs and may require greater efforts, but they

---

35. Schultz, *Transforming Traditional Agriculture*, pp. 5, 16, 48-49, 102-9, 143.
36. Wilfred Malenbaum appraises the Asian potential in these terms. In his view the foremost requirements are motivation and leadership dedicated to progress. See Malenbaum, "Economic Factors and Political Development," *Annals of the American Academy of Political and Social Science* (March 1965), p. 41; "The Asian Economic Potential," ibid. (July 1958), p. 18; *Prospects for Indian Development*, pp. 32-39, 230-33, 295-311.

would still be within the reach of many villages. The growing of new crops, the use of some fertilizer, modest irrigation
facilities, some measures of pest control—all are possibilities
in this category.

Furthermore, there is also the nonagricultural sector to be
considered. At the inexpensive level there are such things as
the breeding of cattle and hogs, the raising of poultry by
more efficient methods, the utilization of milk for dairy products, the keeping of bees, etc. Then there are opportunities
in small scale commerce, in the practice of some trades such
as baking and masonry, and even in sewing and embroidering. Of course a small dose of new knowledge and modest
investments may be required, but again these are well within
the means of the villages themselves.

At a slightly more expensive level there is the development
of cottage industries. Here more equipment is required, as
well as know-how, but it is unnecessary to build a large
plant at once. Some cottage industries seem viable even when
the equipment is simple and the scale of operation small.
Other activities in this category include corn milling, gasoline stations, bottling of soft drinks, ice cream making, and
small scale transportation.

It needs to be emphasized that most of the suggested agricultural and nonagricultural innovations involve, more than
anything else, the propagation of practices already familiar to
some peasants. What is required, more than outside material
assistance, is training, encouragement, and some supervision.
Leadership and motivation have played important roles, and
without them the historical record would have been poorer;
however, they cannot take the place of the technical guidance
that is needed to make the peasants fully aware of the potential of their villages. New and better ways of doing things
must be taught, and the peasants must be convinced that it
is in their interest to try them. All the villages have a representative of the modern sector—the school teacher. If in
addition to educating the young, he could also impart some

simple technical guidance to the adults, and if in addition to being a teacher he were also an enthusiast for progress, many villages could be set in the direction of higher achievements. Furthermore, if the educated native sons took greater interest in the betterment of those whom they left behind and acted accordingly, another step would have been taken in overcoming the lack of technical guidance.

While the exploitation of these untapped possibilities goes forth in the traditional sector, the modern sector will not be standing still. There is a long period ahead during which the absolute difference in per capita income between the two sectors will be increasing. Furthermore, it must be realized that while it is true that the villages have had a superior relative growth, this growth may have been in part due to a "small base effect"—which simply means that at low developmental levels high relative gains are not difficult to achieve. Growth can occur at a self-accelerating rate because so many investment opportunities are available that those which are actually undertaken can be highly productive. In other words, if the development base is small, the costs of growth are relatively low, the investments have very high yields, and these investments are divisible into small amounts without losing their high yields. As growth occurs the prime investment opportunities are exhausted, and if the growth is to be maintained, costlier and less divisible investments must be undertaken.

This does not mean that inexpensive, moderately expensive, and expensive investments must take place simultaneously. The smaller and less developed villages can initially find room for action along the lines indicated above. Having as points of departure low income bases, possibly they can outperform the modern sector in terms of relative growth for some time to come. This is not impossible because these villages will be operating on the self-accelerating portion of their growth curves, so to speak. However, their superior relative growth must be sustained. Otherwise they could achieve considerable progress without greatly reducing the absolute per capita income gap. At higher developmental levels inexpensive innovations and the small base effect will not be working for the villages, and sustained growth will be harder to achieve. It could be said, in a manner of speaking, that the inflection point of their growth curve will then be near and that thereafter the self-retarding portion will appear. This means that somewhat more expensive innovations will be required to maintain the momentum. They would involve higher costs, but they would also make much greater contributions to output.

Some possibilities for expensive innovations can be singled out. In agriculture it would mean imitating the changes that took place in Tepoztlán. This means that not only would new crops be introduced and fertilizer used but that there would be an adoption of such practices as the use of tractors, fumigation, etc.

It will probably be granted that this level of innovation is feasible, but it may be thought that the costs would be prohibitive. This is not necessarily the case, for as the example of Tepoztlán shows even the purchase of tractors can be financed by the savings of the households. On the one hand, a tractor (or truck) need not be paid in one lump sum, and on the other, it is unnecessary to own a large plot of land to make its operation profitable: a tractor can be hired to plow somebody else's land.

There is, however, a serious constraint to progress in agriculture and this is the dependency on rainfall. All the modern practices mentioned above will turn to naught if either it rains so much as to cause flooding or so little as to be a drought. Fortunately, even this difficulty does not involve unsurmountable costs. It will be recalled that even in Chan Kom wells have been dug and water pumps have been installed, but these practices need to become widely adopted. In a sense what the villages need to do is to imitate the modern agricultural sector. They cannot of course match the latter's output, but they can approach its yields. To illustrate, some of the irrigated ejido plots in the modern agricultural sector produced in the middle fifties an average of 2,000 kilograms of corn per hectare;[37] Tepoztlán, as table 32 shows, has already brought its yield up to 1,624 kilograms per hectare and further improvement is possible. It is estimated that in the modern sector improved seed can raise the yield to 3,000–4,000 kilograms per hectare, and such yields may be difficult to match; but if small scale private irrigation is coupled to some of the simpler innovations suggested, the villages should be able to raise their average corn yield close to 2,000 kilograms per hectare. This is not unrealistic because the villages themselves have shown that such yields are entirely possible.[38] In years gone by the productivity of the land has been greater,[39] and therefore to some extent the reversal of the trend involves nothing more than recouping lost ground.

Here again, the possibilities in the nonagricultural sector must not be overlooked. The population increase will make it difficult to provide land for all the would-be farmers. This is a problem that already can be detected in Tepoztlán and to a lesser extent in Mitla. The problem, in fact, is national; even if all the agricultural land were distributed, an efficient agricultural sector may not offer room for all the farm labor.[40] The man-land ratio of the modern agricultural sector is already high,[41] and therefore it does not seem likely

37. Corn is not an important crop in the modern agricultural sector, but small amounts are cultivated.
38. It may be remembered that in Mitla (see chap. 4) land close to the streams produces 1,500 kg. of corn per ha. whereas land dependent on rainfall produces only 300 kg. per ha., and that land seemingly unproductive can be brought under cultivation when irrigated.
39. This has clearly been the case in the smaller villages although even in Tepoztlán, land which now produces close to 2,500 kg. of corn per ha. used to produce only 900 kg. before modernization.
40. See *El mercado de valores* (Mexico), 21 March 1966, p. 251.
41. In some respects the man-land ratio of the modern agricultural sector does not seem to be much different from that of the villages; its advantage lies on the economies of scale achieved either by cultivating collectively sev-

that the government would allow that sector to absorb labor from the poor regions, or do anything that might interfere with its productivity.[42] Hence, if an inefficient system of minifundia is to be avoided, the nonagricultural potential must also be tapped. Besides, nonagricultural activities are profitable. As table 32 shows, nonagricultural income can be larger than agricultural income. Too, more women are entering the labor force, and it is necessary to create for them nonfarm sources of employment.

Some of the opportunities open in the more costly nonagricultural area include such undertakings as the exploitation of quarries in Mitla and the establishment of a small cannery in the vicinity of Tepoztlán. The latter could absorb the output of tomatoes, and other vegetables, from the surrounding region, thereby preventing their rotting on the ground when low prices make unprofitable their shipment to Mexico City. Needless to say, neither of the two possibilities mentioned needs to be carried out on a grand scale. Both appear profitable, although they may entail higher risks and probably outside participation.

Up to this point the major burden of growth will rest on the villages' shoulders. But even after the costly innovations

---

eral small plots, or by cultivating individually a large plot. Large ejidos are worked collectively. In 1955 the average amount of land per ejido holder was 4.54 ha.—a figure somewhat below the average of 4.8 ha. shown by table 32 for the villages. There is also private tenure in the modern sector, and in this case the size of the average plot is 14.87 ha. It is reported that in the modern private plots agriculture is more mechanized and that they have the highest productivity in the country; also that there are holdings, especially in the northwest part of the country, that exceed 800 ha. See *Los Distritos de reigo del noroeste* (Mexico: Centro de Investigaciones Agrarias, 1957), p. 1.
42. The modern agricultural sector appears to have high priority. To it the federal government commits large investment funds. The pay-off from these investments has been large as this sector has responded with impressive output increases which have made possible not only larger consumption of food by a growing population but also important foreign exchange earnings, mainly through the export of wheat and cotton. An idea of the pay-off can be gathered from the output increases mentioned in chapter 3 since they occurred mainly in the modern sector. It may be added that between 1945 and 1955, whereas industrial production increased 80 percent, agricultural production increased 117.6 percent.

are introduced there will still be a potential to be tapped. Here, however, more serious problems need to be faced. The specter of indivisibilities raises its head. Projects appear on the horizon, but for them outside inputs emerge as a real need. Tepoztlán has some lands that become flooded almost every year, and for this reason they are cultivated only after the rainy season. If flood control facilities were built, this land could probably produce two crops a year; but a project of this nature, although quite modest in comparison with the undertakings of the federal government in the modern agricultural sector, would certainly be beyond the resources of the villages. And it is not likely that it could effectively be built by piecemeal efforts on the part of the farmers. Yet, a project of this sort could help to supply a growing population with food and could also help to reduce Tepoztlán's unemployment problem.

Is it at this point that government aid becomes critical? If the villages have been doing well—either because of the small base effect or because of their internal dynamism— why does the government need to come into the picture? If the villages are following a converging path toward the nation's income level, what reason is there to believe that they will not continue to do so?

Taking the last question first, it is perhaps clear that even if it assumed that the projected rates of growth will continue into the future, a realistic closing of the gap will not occur for a long time to come. It needs to be kept in mind that a high rate of growth of the traditional sector is not enough, it must be clearly superior to that of the modern sector and it must not falter. The problem here is that when villages reach the developmental level of Tepoztlán, they seem to run into obstacles that make difficult the maintenance of a high rate of growth.

Hence, it is not suggested that government aid might go to all the villages at the same time. Villages at low developmental levels have inexpensive untapped possibilities that can be exploited with little government aid. However, when barriers begin to make growth difficult, then government assistance can help to overcome them. This assistance would not be something new because, after all, the government has already played an important role in the development of the villages. To its credit, the government seems to be aware of the wide-ranging consequences which neglect of the traditional sector could unleash, and it also seems to realize that the poor areas are as much part of the country as modern Mexico City and that any program of national development that does not include them cannot get very far. The villages, moreover, need not be mere recipients of aid. They do not come to the government empty-handed. As the discussion at the end of chapter 3 made clear, they already make large contributions toward the support of government and they could contribute even more through an integrated system of taxation aimed not toward maximum revenue on the short run but toward maximum growth on the long run. Moreover, as villages develop they will be placed in a position of becoming more capable taxpayers. Thus it seems that when the villages come to a barrier that strains them beyond the limit of their capabilities, what they need, more than government aid per se, is a planning, administrative, transfering agency that will take their tax-paying capacity and direct it toward those projects which—either because of technological complexity or because of indivisibilities, etc.— the villages cannot undertake themselves.

To say that government can fulfill this function is not to imply that the function needs to be provided permanently. It is only needed at critical junctures to assure that the growth of the traditional sector is sustained. For if the cannery is not started, nobody else will come to the villages' rescue. It is to be hoped that the channels of equalization will be doing their job, but as Hicks points out, not too much should be claimed for them, particularly when the one seemingly most effective—labor migration—is the one that should be relied on least.

In deliberate participation by government, the welfare of the traditional sector is obviously involved, but the welfare of the nation is also involved. Lack of greater concern toward the rural areas could result in a modern sector forging ahead while the traditional sector is slowed down by barriers and ceilings that it should be able to overcome. Were it to fail in this task the situation would be risky indeed. For it should be noted that the traditional sector is much larger than the statistics would have one believe. Supposedly, Mexico is only 49 percent rural, but the rural classification ends at the 2,500 population level, a figure surely too low to effect a meaningful rural-urban separation. A rural sector encompassing around 66 percent of the population is closer to reality.[43] The problem is that for this large number of people there is room neither in the modern agricultural sector nor in industry. As already mentioned, in the former the influx of additional farmers could not but reduce its productivity, and the latter is too small to absorb large numbers of workers.[44]

The study should not end on a dissonant note. There is a bright side to the story. The growth of the traditional sector presents problems, but it also presents opportunities. One that should be obvious is a reciprocal or supplementary relationship with respect to the modern sector. The traditional sector has needs, but it also has potential customers, it has potential taxpayers, and it has human resources that can be rallied to the cause of progress.

43. The 1960 census breaks down the total population by political entities. The cities account for 34 percent of the total, the remainder being distributed among villages, towns, and smaller political entities. See *VIII Censo general de población, resumen general* (Mexico: Dirección General de Estadística, 1962), table 4, p. 52.
44. According to the 1960 census, industry employed only 19 percent of the labor force; agriculture was the most important sector, employing 54.1 percent. Industry, moreover, will not be able to offer mass employment until it has reached a rather large size—particularly if it introduces labor-saving methods.

Appendix

A Note on the Measurement of Interregional Inequality

A. *Regional Aggregations*

The way in which a particular spatial aggregation can affect the measurement of interregional inequality can be illustrated by examining some data for Brazil.[1] In 1960 the impoverished multistate region of Brazil known as the Northeast had a per capita income that was 51 percent of the national average. The corresponding figure for the rich multistate region known as the South was 146 percent, i.e., the interregional per capita income differential was 2.8 to 1 between the South and the Northeast. At the state level, however, the per capita income of the poor Northeastern state of Piaui was 29 percent of the nation's average whereas the corresponding figure for the rich southern state of Sao Paulo was 178 percent. This means that at the state level the differential jumps from 2.8 to 6.1. This result is of course to be expected since the multistate aggregation, by taking in disparate numbers, cannot but introduce some averaging.

B. *Population as a Factor in Regional Income Comparisons*

The difference introduced by population when comparisons between regions are made using income as the unit of measurement can readily be seen when the comparison involves changes through time. Additional data for Brazil, presented in table 35, can make this clear.

The figures in the table are self-explanatory, but attention may be called to the last row. The second and third columns

1. These data are taken from S. H. Robock, *Brazil's Developing Northeast: A Study of Regional Planning and Foreign Aid* (Washington: Brookings Institution, 1963) table 2.5, p. 36.

TABLE 35

Changes in Income Differentials between Two

Brazilian Regions, 1950-60

REGIONS	TOTAL INCOME[a]		PER CAPITA INCOME[a]	
	1950	1960	1950	1960
South	48.2	50.7	151	146
Northeast	16.4	15.9	48	51
Difference[b]	31.8	34.8	103	95

SOURCE: Data from Robock, *Brazil's Developing Northeast*, tables 2.3, 2.4, and 2.5, pp. 34-36. Further data can be found in W. Baer, "Regional Inequality and Economic Growth in Brazil," *Economic Development and Cultural Change* 12, no. 3 (April 1964), tables 2 and 5, pp. 272, 276.
[a] The figures are percentages using the corresponding national figures as 100.
[b] Percentage points.

show that between 1950 and 1960 the difference between the total income of the South and the total income of the Northeast increased from 31.8 to 34.8 percentage points. The next two columns, on the other hand, show that on a per capita basis the difference declined from 103 to 95 percentage points. As might be suspected, these opposite trends are explained by the intervening population changes of the two regions. The Northeast sustained heavy out-migration, some of which went into the South, the net effect being that the population growth rate of the Northeast was lower than that of the South and as a result the Northeast had a greater growth rate of per capita income.

An example of a country where the interregional disparity appears more pronounced in terms of per capita income than in terms of total income is Italy. Here this reversal is caused by the population increase of the poor region (the South) being greater than that of the rich region (the Northeast).[2]

2. See Lloyd Saville, "Sectional Developments in Italy and the United States," *Southern Economic Journal* 23, no. 1 (July 1956), p. 43; United Nations, Department of Economic and Social Affairs, *Economic Survey of Europe in 1954,* p. 142; R. S. Eckaus, "The North-South Differential in Italian Economic Development," *Journal of Economic History* 21, no. 3 (September 1961), p. 285; and H. B. Chenery, "Development Policies for Southern Italy," *Quarterly Journal of Economics* 76, no. 4 (November 1962), p. 515.

Index

Asterisk (*) indicates further references under each village heading: Chan Kom; Mitla; Soteapan; Tepoztlán.

*Agriculture: in Mexico, 24–25, 63, 103, 205–6; and savings, 172; surplus labor in, 15–16.

*Animals, 25, 39–40, 46, 49, 50.

*Barter, 25, 40–41.

Base period, identified, 20; surveys of, 21, table 1. *See also* Mexico, conditions in the thirties

Beans: cultivation of, 45–47, 105, 108; importance of, 23–24, 45, 49, 112.

Benedict, F. G., on the diet of the Maya Indians, 50 n. 68

Berry, B. J. L., on primacy of cities, 3 n

Boake, J. H., theory of dualism, 4

Brazil: interregional inequality, 5–7, 196 n, 211–12; movement of capital in, 185

Browning, C. E., on primacy of cities, 3 n

Capital, as channel of equalization, 9, 185–86; requirements of, for economic development, 201

Chan Kom: agriculture, 38, 42, 48–49, 57, 105–7, 115, 132, 136, 138–39, 160, 177, *tables* 8, 32; animals, 92–93, 133–34, 140;

assets of households sampled, 132–34, 138, *table* 18; attitudes, 134, 136, 168, 170; barter, 40; clothing, 137–38, 161–62, *table* 20; communal labor, 53, 54, 70, 74, 98, 99–100; communications, 27, 69–70, *table* 2; culture, 32, 74–75, *tables* 4, 11; demographic characteristics, 28, 66, 67–68, 105–6, 187, *tables* 3, 5, 9, 10; expenditures of households sampled, 137–41, 161–63, *tables* 20, 21; feasts, 59, 170–71; food, 49, 59, 105–6, 137–38, 161–63, *table* 20; founding of, 26 n; general characteristics of households sampled, 131–32, *table* 17; geographical characteristics, 35, 36, 48–49, 175, *tables* 2, 5, 6; government, 53, 75, 98; house furnishings, 51; housing, 50, 93–94, 132, *table* 18; income of households sampled, 135–37, *table* 19; investments, 106–7, 136, 140, 141, *table* 21; land tenure, 42, 43, 105, 106; leadership, 68, 70, 74, 83, 98, 168; nonagricultural activities, 38, 92–94, 175, *table* 7; opportunities for output expansion, 198, 199; personality

213